Timely Rain

TIMELY RAIN

Selected Poetry of Chögyam Trungpa

EDITED BY *David I. Rome*

SHAMBHALA
Boston
1998

Shambhala Publications, Inc.
Horticultural Hall
300 Massachusetts Avenue
Boston, Massachusetts 02115
http://www.shambhala.com

First Edition
Printed in the United States
⊗ This edition is printed on acid-free paper that meets
the American National Standards Institute Z39.48 Standard.

Distributed in the United States by Random House, Inc.,
and in Canada by Random House of Canada Ltd

Library of Congress Cataloging-in-Publication Data
Trungpa, Chogyam, 1939–
    Timely rain: selected poetry of Chögyam Trungpa/
    edited by David I. Rome.—1st ed.
       p.   cm.—(Shambhala centaur editions)
    ISBN 1-57062-174-8 (acid-free paper)
    1. Buddhist poetry, American.   I. Rome, David I.   II. Title.
    III. Series.
    PS3570.R84A6   1998   97-32056   811'.54—dc21   CIP

Contents

Introduction
by Allen Ginsberg

As LINEAGE HOLDER in Ear-whispered Kagyü transmission of Tibetan Buddhist practice of Wakefulness, Chögyam Trungpa is "Rinpoche" or "Precious Jewel" of millennial practical information on attitudes and practices of mind speech & body that Western Poets over the same millennia have explored, individually, fitfully, as far as they were able—searching thru cities, scenes, seasons, manuscripts, libraries, backalleys, whorehouses, churches, drawing rooms, revolutionary cells, opium dens, merchant's rooms in Harrar, salons in Lissadell.

Rimbaud, drawing on the Magician Eliphas Levi & hashishien backalleys of Paris, rediscovered "Alchemy of the Verb" and other Western magics including

Editor's Note: Allen Ginsberg, a devoted student of Chögyam Trungpa Rinpoche since 1971, intended to write an introduction for this book. His sudden death in April of 1997, ten years to the day after Trungpa's own passing, prevented this. By kind permission of Allen Ginsberg's executors, we have reprinted the above essay which originally appeared in 1983 as the introduction to *First Thought Best Thought,* an earlier collection of Trungpa's poems.

home-made Colors of Vowels & "long reasoned derangement of all the senses" as part of his scheme to arrive at the Unknown as Poet-seer. His conception of Poet as Visionary Savant is unbeatable ambition no Western poet can bypass, tho as in the lives of Rimbaud & Kerouac, mature suffering, the First Noble Truth of existence, may be the destined end of ambitious magic. Some Reality is arrived at: "Charity is that key—This inspiration proves that I have dreamed! . . . I who called myself angel or seer, exempt from all morality, I am returned to the soil with a duty to seek and rough reality to embrace! Peasant!"

Rimbaud, still a model of the Beautiful Poet, concluded his life's last year with the following letters: "In the long run our life is a horror, an endless horror! What are we alive for?" . . . "My life is over, all I am now is a motionless stump." Generations later poets are still trying to change Reality with the Revolution of the Word, a XX Century preoccupation drawing on Western gnostic sources.

Some compromise with Absolute Truth had to be made in XX Century poets: W. C. Williams thru Kerouac, poets were willing to work with relative truth, the sight at hand, accurate perception of appearance, accurate reportage of consciousness—although Hart Crane & some Rock Poets continued to force the issue of Self-Immolation as means of becoming One with phenomena.

As part of the aesthetics of working with relative truth, an American can idiom developed (born out of the spacious pragmatism of Whitman in dealing with his own Ego): The acceptance of actual poetic (poesis: making) behavior of the mind as model, subject, & measure of literary form and content. Mind is shapely, Art is shapely. Gertrude Stein's style thus merges literary artifact with present consciousness during the time of composition. Put another way: the sequence of events of poet's mind, accidents of mind, provide the highlights, jumps & Plot of Poetry. As to the Muse, "She's there, installed amid the kitchenware" as Whitman celebrated the change from Absolute Heroic to Relative Honesty in poetic method. Thus we inherited our world of poetry in XX Century.

Thirst for some Absolute Truth still lurks behind this shift, thus Bullfighting, Drugs, God, Communism, Realpolitik or Revolution, Drink, Suburb or Bohemia, Sex, grassroots communalism, ecology or Amerindian ground, blasts of Eternal Vision, Death's Skull, even various Apocalypses or Extraterrestrial Paranoias & delights recur as our preoccupation, and have been epic'd. Brave energies of fear, joy or anomia, not much certainty; yet there's been honest effort to display what can be seen of naked mind, and that's led to an amazingly open style of Poetry, which includes snow-blinding Sierras and rain-diamonded traffic lights, as mind's-eye does. An international style, based on facts, has emerged, perhaps that most relaxed poetic mode ever. Still, no certainty emerges but ultimate suffering, accelerating change, and perhaps some vast glimpse of universal soullessness. Has the poetic Seer failed? Or perhaps succeeded at arriving at a place of beat bleakness where the ego of Poetry is annihilated?

At last! To the Rescue! Carrying the panoply of 25 centuries of wakened mind-consciousness "where glorious radiant Howdahs / are being carried by elephants / through groves of flowing milk / past paradises of Waterfall / into the valley of bright gems / be rubying an antique ocean / floor of undiscovered splendor / in the heart of un happiness."* And Whozat? The poet of absolute Sanity and resolution, "having drunk the hot blood of the ego." The author is a reincarnated Tibetan Lama trained from age 2 in various ancient practices aimed at concentrating attention, focusing perception, minding thought-forms to transparency, profounding awareness, vasting consciousness, annihilating ego, & immolating ego-mind in phenomena: a wizard in control of day-dream, conscious visualization & thought projection, vocal sound vibration, outward application of insight, practice of natural virtues, and a very admiral of oceanic scholarship thereof.

*That's Kerouac's Wish-fulfilling gem, *Mexico City Blues*, 110th Chorus, (New York: Grove Press, 1959).

The dramatic situation of someone who has realized the World as pure mind, & gone beyond attachment to ego to return to the world & work with universal ignorance, confront the spiritual-materialist daydream of Western world—and tell it in modernist poetry—provides the historic excitement this book puts in our laps.

To focus on one aspect of the drama, consider the progression of style, from early poems adapted out of Tibetan formal-classic modes, to the free-wheeling Personism improvisations of the poems of 1975, which reflect Guru mind's wily means of adapting techniques of Imagism, post-surrealist humor, modernist slang, subjective frankness & egoism, hip "fingerpainting," & tenderhearted spontaneities as adornments of tantric statement. We see respect & appreciation given to the "projective field" of modern Western poetry; this is a teaching in itself, which few past "Gurus" have been able to manifest in their mistier mystic musings. Something has jerked forward here, into focus, visible, in our own language: rare perceptions dealt with in our own terms.

By hindsight the classical style poems become precious exhibitions of cultural starting place & intention for the poet, Chögyam, "the stray dog."

For those familiar with advanced Buddhist practice & doctrine, the solidified symbolisms of early poems are significant teachings, or statements of method, attitude, & experience, as in "The Zen Teacher," where horse, boat and stick may represent Hinayana Mahayana & Vajrayana attitudes of wakefulness. Quite thrilling, unusual, to find a contemporary poet who's master of an ancient "system." Within my memory, it was Academically fashionable to say that the XX Century lacked the culture for great Poetry, not possessing, as Dante's time did, a "system" of cultural assumptions on which to hang an epic. But it seemed too late to go back and clothe the skeleton of God, tho Eliot, Claudel & others yearned nostalgic for such divine certainty.

Chögyam Trungpa, however, does have a Classical system working for him to make "the snakeknot of conceptual mind uncoil in air." Vajrayana Buddhist symbolism is at his disposal, including the notion of "Absolute Truth"—a property hitherto unclaimable since Plato kicked the poets out of his republic. Tho' Keats did propose redeeming Truth as Beauty. Blake created a symbolic sacred world in many ways parallel to Vajrayana. How do other poet friends look in this light, faced with contest from within their ranks by poet who's also lineage holder of the most esoteric teachings in the East? Will Auden seem amateur, pursuing testy quasi-christian personal conclusions? Does

Eliot quote Buddha, Krishna & Christ like a country vicar? How do I sit, charlatan pedant full of resentful Ginsberghood, posed by contemporary media as cultural Guru? Does Yeats gasp like a beached fish in the thin air of Theosophy's "Secret Doctrines" version of the Great East? Whereas "Chögyam writing a poem is like a king inspecting his Soldiers." Well, Well!

What will poetry readers think of that bardic boast? Diamond Macho the *Kalevala* song men wouldn't match, tho' they might threaten to sing each other into a swamp.* What image of Poet! What would angelic Shelly've said? What would Blake warn? "I must make a system of my own, or be enslaved by another man's"? On Mt. Ida the Muses look up astonished by this bolt of lightning thru blue cloudless sky.

This book is evidence of a Buddha-natured child taking first verbal steps age 35, in totally other language direction than he spoke age 10, talking side of mouth slang: redneck, hippie, chamber of commerce, good citizen, Oxfordian aesthete slang, like a dream Bodhisattva with thousand eyes & mouths talking turkey.

Thus poems of June 1972 approach the theme of personal love using open Western forms and "first

* *The Kalevala,* tr. F. P. MaGoun Jr. (Cambridge, Mass.: Harvard University Press, 1963), poem 3, 21–330 ". . . up to his teeth behind a rotten tree trunk."

thought best thought" improvisatory technique—statements which mediate between the formality of Dharma Master and a man immersed in Relative Truth. Phrases return and re-echo in mind: "Take a thistle to bed, / And make love to it." The following "Letter to Marpa," classical theme, is done in smooth mixture of old and new styles: "Ordering Damema to serve beer for a break." If you know the wife of Marpa (translator and early founder of Kagyü Lineage) & Trungpa Rinpoche, this poem's a historic prophecy of transplantation of lineage to America in American terms: awesome knowledge & self-aware humor are explicit in the poem.

"Nameless Child": "hearing the pearl dust crunch between his teeth" is a startling statement of egolessness, "unborn nature" of consciousness, done in traditional style. The next experiment is with gnomic haiku-like riddles, developing 7 November 1972 into precise American style "red wheelbarrow" snapshots. "Skiing in a red & blue outfit, drinking cold beer," etc. Thru these we see ordinary mind of the poet, whose specialty as Eastern Teacher is Ordinary Mind.

Years later ordinary egoless mind says in response to anxiety-ridden ecology freaks, "Glory be to the rain / That brought down / Concentrated pollution / On the roof of my car / In the parking lot." Amazing chance to see his thought process step by step, link by link, cutting through solidifications of opinion & fixations on "Badgoodgood/goodbadbad" & attachment to this and that humorless image the poems July 1974, including "Ginsberg being Pedantic."

This method of first-thought concatenations develops in a series of tipsy essays in modern style—some dealing with serious personal matters. By September 1974, in "Supplication to the Emperor," Ancient Wisdom Transmission heritage is wedded to powerful modern "surrealist" style.

These poems are dictated amidst an ocean of other activities including the utterance of masses of books of Dharma exposition—as the Tibetan imagery says "a mountain of jewels"—exactly true of this strange poet in our midst, noticing our "Aluminum-rim black leather executive chairs."

What's odd, adventurous, inventive, mind-blowing, is the combination of classical occasion (visit of head of Kagyü Order, His Holiness Gyalwa Karmapa, to North America) treated in authentic post-Apollinaire recognizably American-minded style ("Supplication to the Emperor").

Poignant and powerful then, the re-echoes of liturgical style that reappear in 1974, the poet in midst of struggle with the flypaper of modern centerless-minded poetics: (as in an unpublished text, "Homage to Samantabhadra," 11 November 1974)

I am a mad Yogi.
Since I have no beginning, no end,
I am known as the ocean of Dharma.
I am the primordial madman;
I am primordially drunk.
Since all comes from me,
I am the only son of the only Guru.

By February 1975, a series of poems in entirely modern style indicate absorption of the lively fashion of versifying developed in the U.S. after models of Christopher Smart & Apollinaire, & transmitted in U.S. '50s to '70s by Corso, the "List Poem" spoken of by Anne Waldman and others—see the cadenzas punning and joking on the world Palm (25 February 1975), the "best minds" commentary of the same day, and subsequent love poems. In "Dying Laughing" there's an ironic commentary on modern poetic mind, "scattered thoughts are the best you can do . . . That the whole universe / could be exasperated / And die laughing."

There follows a series of portraits—"characters" as T. S. Eliot termed certain of W. C. Williams' poems on persons—thumbnail sketches of his students, their natures exposed to X-ray humorous advice—"If you're going to tickle me, be gentle . . . But titillating enough to stimulate my system with your feminine healthy shining well-trimmed nail just so . . ."

Of the famous situation of Guru playing with disciples this is rare honest private occasion made public where you can see the inside story & its humanity & innocence, its true teaching & bone quick insight. Tiny details of personality, irritating seen in greater space, along with tiny details of resolution of problems of egoic self-consciousness proposed by subjects of the portraits—this one composed March 1975:

> . . . jalapeño dumpling
> Bitten by Alice's white teeth,
> Which are lubricated by feminine saliva

There's an odd reminder of Kurt Schwitters' *Anne Blume* here, or: the love poem dated 7 March 1975:

> As she turns her head
> From the little irritation of long flowing hair
> She says, Mmmm.
> But on the other hand she is somewhat perturbed;
> Not knowing whether she is glamorous or ugly

A number of successful complete poems follow, the poetic ground having been prepared, the improvisational practice having been taken seriously, thus "Victory Chatter" is fruition of poetic path begun consciously much earlier. The details in the mind of the "good general" of dharma battle are recognizable. A number of poems like "Missing the Point" have extra flavor of inside gossip on attitudes & thought processes of the professional teacher, "Lingering thought / Tells me / My private secretary is really drunk" & have sort of Chinese Royal tone; might've been written in 14th Century Kham slang. "RMDC": "Dead or alive, I have no regrets." An up-to-date playfulness develops, mind-plays of obvious charm, even naivete, as in writings by Marsden Hartley or Samuel Greenberg's not-well-known classics.

"Report from Loveland," July 1975: The whole dharma is given in Disneyesque parody of everyday perplexity's Bourgeois life. By that month's end, the writings are well-formed shapes with one subject. The "1135 10th St." lady friend poem is a series of exquisitely courteous & penetrant, yet funny, first thoughts, where minds mixed with dharma and every noticed detail points in a unified direction. Can you, by following first thoughts, arrive at a rounded complete one-subject poem, but crazy-poetic still, like: "fresh air / Which turns into a well-cared-for garden / Free from lawn-mowers and insecticides?"

In "Aurora 7 #2" the poet emerges complete whole, teacher & self, talking to the world his world, face to face, completely out of the closet poetically so to speak, without losing poetic dignity as Tantrick Lama & Guru: "Here comes Chögyie / Chögyie's for all / Take Chögyie as yours / Chögyam says: lots of love! / I'm yours!"

I must say, that there is something healthy about the American idiom as it's been charmed into being by Williams, Kerouac, Creeley and others, a frankness of person & accuracy to thought-forms & speech that may've been unheard of in other cultures, a freestyle stick-your-neck-out mortal humor of the "Far West." When the Great East enters this body speech & mind there is a ravishing combination of Total Anarchy & Total Discipline.

Well, has the transition been made, by this poet, from Absolute Truth expressed thru symbols ("riding on the white horse of Dharmata")* to Relative Truth nail'd down in devotional commitment to the American Ground he's set out to transvalue & conquer?—In the drama of this book, yes, the author Chögyam, with all his Vajra Perfections, is the drunk poet on his throne in the Rockies proclaiming "Chögyie is yours." What will Walt Whitman's expansive children do faced with such a Person?

LAND O'LAKES, 1976
BOULDER, 1983

* *Rain of Wisdom*, tr. by Nalanda Translation, Committee (Boulder & London: Shambhala Publications, 1980), p. 285, "The Spontaneous Song of the White Banner" by Chögyam Trungpa.

PART ONE

The Silent Song of Loneliness

Silk Road

A herd of sheep roam on the meadows ornamented
 with turquoise flowers;
The crow caws on the pine branch, conversing easily
 with the magpie.
Flags flutter on a cairn, on a red rock peak where
 vultures nest.
From a black tent amidst dark old yak folds smoke
 rises gently,
And the conches and drums of invited lamas echo in
 the distance—
Irrepressibly happy and sad to see the highlands of the
 snow land Tibet.

Traveling, listening to the whistling wind, crossing
 thousands of ridges but still not seeing the end of
 the earth;
Irritated by the gossip of the brooks, crossing
 thousands of rivers but still not reaching the end of
 the sky;
Never reaching the goal of the nomad's black tent in
 the distance—
It is too tiring for the horses and mules: better to pitch
 our tent where pasture, water and firewood are
 plentiful.

Tibetan Pilgrim

On the right, a mountain with juniper trees—at its
   foot a farmhouse topped with white prayer flags—is
   like a minister on a tigerskin seat.
On the left, a mountain covered with tamarisk
   trees—at its foot a farm filled with beautiful green
   wheat and barley—is like a queen on a silken throne.
Straight ahead, a rocky mountain rises above a
   monastery with glittering gold roofs like a king on a
   throne of gold.
An old pilgrim feasts his eyes on the richness of some
   merchant's camp, and patiently continues towards
   Lhasa.

The red flag flies above the Potala

The red flag flies above the Potala,
The people of Tibet are drowned in an ocean of blood;
A vampire army fills the mountains and plains,
But self-existing dignity never wanes.

Song of the Golden Elephant

The eagle soars away into the sky
And yet he never plumbs the depths of space.
The four seasons give place to one another,
Yet never seem to have an end or a beginning.
When the one dry tree on the hill is blown down
By the timely wind, what can one do?

The whistling winter wind blows lightly
The white flowers of the snow-flakes.
Remembering the mother herding yaks,
How can one ever forget the highland of Gejê?

O pillar of the sky, high mountain peak,
Hills, where trees and grasses grow, surround you,
Yet you remain alone and still,
The cloud of peace wrapped round about your
    shoulders.
Remembering the fatherland
The white flag is fluttered by the song of sadness.
The beautiful form of Jomo Lhari mountain
Comes suddenly to mind
And only the liquid turquoise of the lake
Can comfort me.

The East side and the West side of the hill are seen
    together
And the white banner that is thereupon
Speaks of that thing far off yet close at hand.

A young and golden elephant I offer you.
Beware the baby elephant
Still in the jungle,
The lonely child who drinks the hot fresh milk.
When he presents you with a crystal mirror
Make out the golden syllables
Written on my heart.

Read this by the light of the torch that dispels darkness.

from The Silent Song of Loneliness

A sharpness is on the Summer's tail;
The healing breeze of Summer yields
To the bitter wind of Winter time.
If this was a signal to you, bird,
Then you would know the seasons not
Themselves, but as a turning wheel.

The young deer, wandering among
The Summer green and pleasant ways,
Remembering his mother caught
And killed in a trap, can yet enjoy
The freedom of the empty valley
And find relief and rest of mind.

The lonely child who travels through
The fearful waste and desolate fields,
And listens to their barren tune,
Greets as an unknown and best friend
The terror in him, and he sings
In darkness all the sweetest songs.

The lonely bird lived all his days
In a place apart, yet did not know
Peace, or the dwelling-place of peace.

But when the face of loneliness
Is known to you, then you will find
The Himalayan hermitage.

The jungle child sings his song
Sad and alone, yet weeps for nothing,
And joy is in him as he hears
The flute the peaceful wind is blowing.
And even so am I, in the sky
Dancing, riding the wild duck.

Stray Dog

Chögyam is merely a stray dog.
He wanders around the world,
Ocean or snow-peak mountain pass.
Chögyam will tread along as a stray dog
Without even thinking of his next meal.
He will seek friendship with birds and jackals
And any wild animals.

Completely intoxicated by you

Completely intoxicated by you,
This longing for Padma Trimê.
There is nothing to conceal,
Yet hardly anything to expose
For my faith and devotion is beyond word or melody
    of music.
A kind that no one would be able to hear or
    understand.

It is beautiful to grow with this loneliness,
Since it is your aloneness which inspires and drives me
    into selfless action.
The echo of your voice is heard.
The expression of your face is seen.
But when I become acquainted with these,
There is no more longing,
But the infinite compassion is inherited by your son.
You thrust upon me this weight.
I know it will remain as burden
Until I see your face in me,
And hear your voice from everywhere.

This is you Padma Trimê:
Ornamented with yogi costumes,

Dancing on a cloud,
Singing in the language of Dakinis—
You are the fire and water,
You act as the earth and the space
Which accommodate the infinite.

Looking into the world

Looking into the world
I see alone a chrysanthemum,
Lonely loneliness,
And death approaches.
Abandoned by guru and friend,
I stand like the lonely juniper
Which grows among rocks,
Hardened and tough.
Loneliness is my habit—
I grew up in loneliness.
Like a rhinoceros
Loneliness is my companion—
I converse with myself.
Yet sometimes also,
Lonely moon,
Sad and Happy
Come together.

Do not trust.
If you trust you are in
Others' hands.
It is like the single yak
That defeats the wolves.
Herds panic and in trying to flee

Are attacked.
Remaining in solitude
You can never be defeated.
So do not trust,
For trust is surrendering oneself.
Never, never trust.

But be friendly.
By being friendly towards others
You increase your non-trusting.
The idea is to be independent,
Not involved,
Not glued, one might say, to others.
Thus one becomes ever more
Compassionate and friendly.
Whatever happens, stand on your own feet
And memorise this incantation:
Do not trust.

Red glaring from the West

Red glaring from the West
Sound of raindrops—
Such a peculiar climate
And a rainbow, too.
Freedom,
Freedom from limitations,
Freedom from the square
(Exact patterns all carefully worked out),
Freedom from mathematical psychology
And logic.
The banner of true and free
Flies in the air of the middle way.
It is somehow wholesome,
Healthy as the energetic tiger
Or lion.
Growl,
GROWL—
Beautiful pointed teeth
Demonstrating invincibility.
I, Chögyam, watch all this
From the top of a pine tree
Bending in the wind
Quite nonchalantly.

Three-bladed missile

Three-bladed missile
Piercing to the sky—
Vroom,
Bang, Bang!
It leaves the ground.
It is the manifestation of hatred
For the whole earth,
Hatred for this whole solar system.
Who is the victim?
Who is the victor?
It is highly ironical
While others live on
Such luxury.
There must be some force of
Truth and justice—
These very words have been over-used.
Yet with the force of the true powerful nature
There will be the perfect situation
Which is unorganised,
Inspired by the pupil who is not conditioned.
So the world is not
All that pitch black—
There is some harmony
And in this harmony we live.

We have been inspired
Yet are neither anarchists
Nor revolutionaries
In the blind sense.
Love to you all.

Whistling grasses of the Esk Valley

Whistling grasses of the Esk Valley,
So many incidents occur.
The image is the climate of this part of the country.
There comes a hailstorm—
Children, children, seek protection!
A mighty thunderbolt strikes to the ground.
It does not make any distinction between trustees and
    the spiritual leader.
Violent winds shake the Scots pine tree,
Copper beech and rhododendrons.
I said to myself,
You, most mighty of all, should have come three weeks
    earlier.
Here is the big storm.
Buckets of rain pour down.
The Esk river turns reddish in color,
Sweeps all the trees and branches away.
A mighty force invades our valley—
Fishes thrown up on the banks for the birds' delight.

Chögyam watches all this,
Wishing that I could be one of those fishes,
That this ruthless political current would throw me
    away.

Why wasn't I born an innocent fish
That could die in peace on the banks of the Esk?
If karma exists the weather will adjust.
I am not seeking revenge.
I am seeking peace
As one of those fish peacefully dead on the bank,
Its body a feast of its victory.
But I cannot help thinking they will say grace before
    the meal,
And will have a good cook
To make their evening feast enjoyable.

In the north of the sky

In the north of the sky there is a great and dark cloud
Just about to release a hailstorm.
Mind, children,
Mind, young puppies and kittens,
That your heads are not injured.
Yet these hailstorms are merely pellets of ice.

There were hundreds of magicians
Who tried to prevent storm and hail.
In the course of time
All the ritual hats, altars and ritual garments
Have been blown away by the force of the hailstorms.

Here comes Chögyam disguised as a hailstorm.
No one can confront him.
It is too proud to say Chögyam is invincible,
But it is true to say he cannot be defeated.
Chögyam is a tiger with whiskers and a confident smile.
This is not a poem of pride
Nor of self-glorification:
But he is what he is.
He escaped from the jaw of the lion.

"Clear away," says the commander,
"You are standing on no-man's land.

We do not want to shoot innocent people."
We cannot alter the path of the shell.
Once the bomb is released it knows its duty;
It has to descend.
Chögyam knows the course of his action.
He could be described as a skillful pilot;
He can travel faster than sound,
Faster than thoughts.
He is like a sharp bamboo dagger
That can exterminate pterodactyls
Or fast moving boa constrictors.

I am not interested in playing games.
But what is a game?
It is a game when you shoot pheasants and deer.
You might say this is the game of the politicians,
Rather like the game of mah-jongg
Or that of chess.
Devoid of these games
I will sail straight through
Like a ship sailing through icebergs.
No one can change Chögyam's course,
His great odyssey.

The world waits,
Squirrels in the forest
And those of the moon

Listening in silence
Amidst gently moving clouds.
There is a force of silence
With energy
Which can never be interrupted.
With conviction and energy
I send my love to you.
I love you.

Goodbye and Welcome

"Goodbye"
"Welcome"
"Glad to meet you"
"How do you do"—
All this I hear
Echoing in the cave of social meeting,
And the echo goes on and on
Until it dies in the mountain depths,
Powerless to reflect.
But O World, O Universe,
My journey to the overseas continent needs no
    copyright,
For it has never been conducted in the same manner.
It is the fresh meeting of man,
The true meeting of living man.
It is the pilgrimage,
The great odyssey which I have never feared,
Since I have not hesitated to flow with the river's
    current.

With blessings and wisdom I write this poem,
As I am free once and for all
In the midst of friends who radiate true love.
Love to you all.

PART TWO

Letter to Marpa

Meteoric iron mountain

Meteoric iron mountain piercing to the sky,
With lightning and hailstorm clouds round about it.
There is so much energy where I live
Which feeds me.
There is no romantic mystique,
There is just a village boy
On a cold wet morning
Going to the farm
Fetching milk for the family.
Foolishness and wisdom
Grandeur and simplicity
Are all the same
Because they live on what they are.
There is no application for exotic wisdom,
Wisdom must communicate
To the men of now.
Dharma is the study of what is
And fulfills the understanding of what is here right
    now.
The ripple expands when you throw the pebble:
It is true, a fact.
That is the point of faith,
Of full conviction,
Which no one can defeat or challenge.

Please, readers,
Read it slowly
So you can feel
That depth of calmness as you read.
Love to you.
I am the Bodhisattva who will not abandon you,
In accordance with my vow.
Compassion to all.

A Letter to Marpa

Solid Marpa
Our father,
The message of the lineage:
You are the breadwinner.
Without your farm we would starve to death.
Fertilizing
Plowing
Sowing
Irrigating
Weeding
Harvesting;
Without your farm we are poverty-stricken.
Your stout body,
Sunburnt face;
Ordering Damema to serve beer for a break;
Evidence of the three journeys you made to India in
    you—
We sympathize with you for your son's death:
It was not the fault of the horse,
It was the seduction of the stirrup in which his foot
    was caught
As his head smashed into the boulders of
    conceptualization.
Yet you produced more sons:

Eagle-like Milarepa who dwells in the rocks,
Snow-lion-like Gampopa whose lair is in the Gampo
    hills,
Elephant-like Karmapas who majestically care for their
    young,
Tiger-like Chögyam roaming in foreign jungles.
As your lineage says, "The grandchildren are more
    accomplished than the parents."
Your garuda egg hatches
As the contagious energy of Mahamudra conquers the
    world.
We are the descendants of lions and garudas.

Supplication to the Emperor

You are a rock
You are our foundation
You can cause a landslide
You can shake the earth
You are all the elements
You burn
You quench thirst
You sustain
You are the creator of turbulent fresh air
You sit like a mountain
The world is your throne
The world is helpless
You and your Kagyü lineage
Are the only living monarchs on earth.

Inter-cosmopolitan politics
International Ballistic Missile
Internal Revenue Service for rich hippie spiritual
    shoppers—
In the Age of Darkness
Your multiple all-pervasive macro-precision dharma-
    insight is so penetrating:
Amidst a flock of black sheep
A flock of black pigeons

A depressed herd of buffaloes
Shaggy polar bears munching vegetables
Black cloud hovering above polluted cities
Aluminum-rim black leather executive chairs
Nouveau-riche articulation getting into the silk and
    satin world
Ex-Catholics reentering because of the promise of the
    Mother Church
Sleepy Jews learning to play the Kabbalah puzzle
Hocus-pocus Hindus trying their best in the Armenian
    evangelical jinglebell
Tea parties' old den of Theosophy filled with chatter of
    the new Messiah
Oakwood-paneled meeting halls with deadly pamphlets
    advertising "That" or "This" trip in their elegant
    language:
This dungeon of dark tunnels where millions are
    trapped
Comparing their entrapments as better than others'.

O Dawn of Karmapa
Are you Avalokiteshvara?
If
Are
Are you
You are
So you

You must be
Come forth
The Dawn of Karmapa
The only living monarch on earth
Be kind to us
We wait for your lion's roar
Tiger's claw
Gentle smile
Ostentatious display of your presence.

You did
You will do
You are doing it
So do it
O Dawn of Karmapa.

RMDC, Route 1, Livermore

In the blue sky with no clouds,
The sun of unchanging mind-essence arises;
In the jungle of pine trees swayed by winds,
The birds of chattering thoughts abide;
Among the boulders of immovable dignity,
The insects of subconscious scheming roam;
In the meditation hall many practice dhyana,
Giving birth to realization free of hope and fear.
Through devotion to the only father guru
The place of dharma has been founded,
Abundant with spiritual and temporal powers:
Dead or alive, I have no regrets.

Timely Rain

In the jungles of flaming ego,
May there be cool iceberg of bodhicitta.

On the racetrack of bureaucracy,
May there be the walk of the elephant.

May the sumptuous castle of arrogance
Be destroyed by vajra confidence.

In the garden of gentle sanity,
May you be bombarded by coconuts of wakefulness.

Afterthought

Such a precious human body,
Difficult to rediscover;
Such precious pain,
Not difficult to discover;
Such an old story
Is by now a familiar joke.
You and I know the facts and the case history;
We have a mutual understanding of each other
Which has never been sold or bought by anyone.
Our mutual understanding keeps the thread of sanity.
Sometimes the thread is electrified,
Sometimes it is smeared with honey and butter;
Nevertheless, we have no regrets.
Since I am here,
Seemingly you are here too.
Let us practice!
Sitting is a jewel that ornaments our precious life.

Fishing Wisely

From the samsaric ocean,
With the net of your good posture,
The fish of your subconscious gossip
Are exposed to the fresh air.
No praise, no blame.
The fish of your subconscious mind
Look for samsaric air,
But they die in coemergent wisdom.

Exposé

Acknowledging Accusations in the Name of Devotion

Remember, O Tusum Khyenpa!
Remember, O Father Karma Pakshi!
Remember, O Tilopa!
Remember, O Naropa!
Remember, O Milarepa!
Remember, O Marpa Lotsawa!
When I remember your kindness and your power,
I am left in the midst of the dark-age dungeon.
When I taste your great bliss
It is as if for the first time,
As if no one had tasted honey before.
When I realize your devotion,
It makes me so lonely.
When I see and experience anything good and
    wonderful,
It reminds me of the Kagyü wisdom and what you have
    sacrificed for us.
When I put on good clothing or see an attractive
    maiden,
When I handle gold or diamond,
I feel great pain and love for your wisdom and exertion.
I can only cry,

Your beauty and exertion and footprints make me so
    sad and full of longing,
Because we are left behind, nowhere,
Unable even to see your footprints in the dust.
How could you do such a thing?
Any mark of elegance or imprint of goodness,
For that matter, anything wicked and raw, confused or
    destructive,
Anything we see makes us feel so sad.
We will cry after the Father Kagyü.
Whether we are attacked or praised,
We do not follow the conventional pattern of hope and
    fear.
Nonetheless, you left us alone.
We feel so sad and lonely.
We want to taste you, smell you—
Where are you?
We cry and we would like to threaten you and say:
Show us your true face, to help us never give up!
In this very bed, on this very cushion, in this very
    room—
If you don't show us your face and tell us,
We will perish in tears and dissolve in misery!
Please come and be with us.
At least look at us the way we are,
Which may not be the best you expect of us,
But we have the greatest devotion,

Beyond your preconceptions.
We will cry and shed our tears until our eyeballs drop
    in the sand dune
And we drown in the ocean of our tears.
O Knower of the Three Times, omniscient,
We have tried and practiced after your example:
Please don't give up.
When we iron our clothes, it is for you.
When we shine our shoes, it is for you.
When we wear jewelry, it is for you.
We do everything because of you;
We have no personal concern.
If we do not realize your dignity and wisdom,
May we rot and dissolve into dust.
We do everything for your sake and because of you.
We are so sad because of you,
We are so joyful because of you.
Father, if you have strength, this is the time to manifest.
I am about to die
And be reborn in crying and laughing at the same time.
Father, please have consideration for us.
We do not do anything for our own sake.
We do everything for the sake of devotion to you.

A Heart Lost and Discovered

If there is no full moon in the sky,
How is it possible to see the reflection in the pond?
If the tiger has sharp claws,
How is it possible not to use them?
How could we bake our bread
If there were no fire?
At the death of the Karmapa we become softened and
    devotional.
It is true,
Those who have never cried in their lives, cry this time,
And shed tears that will water the earth
So we can produce further flowers and greenery.

As skylarks hunt for their prey

As skylarks hunt for their prey,
I am captured by their stillness.

I experience neither thirst nor hunger,
But skylarks captivate my memory.

Whistling arrows on the battlefield remind me of my
    general's bravery:
Should I run away or should I stay?

Buddhism neither tells me the false nor the true:
It allows me to discover myself.

Shakyamuni was so silent:
Should I complain against him?

PART THREE

Samsara and Nirvana

The Zen teacher

The Zen teacher hates the horse
But the horse carries him;
At the river both depend on the boat.

For crossing the mountains
It is better to carry a stick.

Samsara and Nirvana

A crow is black
Because the lotus is white.
Ants run fast
Because the elephant is slow.
Buddha was profound;
Sentient beings are confused.

Gain and Loss

He who has not experienced death
Is like an inexperienced father.
He who has not come to life after death
Is like a man suddenly struck dumb.
He who has never been wise
Is like a youth who has never been beautiful.
The stupid man who becomes wise
Is like a beggar who becomes king.
The dog who becomes master
Is like the victor in the revolution.
The master who becomes a dog
Is like a man who has awakened from a pleasant dream.
Meeting an old friend
Is like reading your own autobiography.
Finding a new friend
Is like composing music.
Chögyam writing a poem
Is like a king inspecting his soldiers.

Cynical Letter

Licking honey from a razor blade,
Eyes of the learned gouged out by books,
The beauty of maidens worn by display,
The warrior dead from not knowing fear—
It is ironical to see the dharma of samsara:
Celebrities deafened by fame,
The hand of the artist crippled by rheumatism.

The moth flew into the oil lamp,
The blind man walks with a torch,
The cripple runs in his wheelchair,
A fool's rhetoric is deep and learned,
The laughing poet
Has run out of breath and died.
The religious spin circles, in accordance with religion;
If they had not practiced their religion, they could not
    spin.
The sinner cannot spin according to religion;
He spins according to not knowing how to spin.
The yogis spin by practicing yoga;
If they don't have chakras to spin, they are not yogis.
Chögyam is spinning, watching the spinning/samsara;
If there is no samsara/spinning, there is no Chögyam.

Philosopher Fool

There is a famous snow mountain capped with mist, like a king wearing a crown. It is said that from this mountain one may see the North and South Poles simultaneously. This mountain is encircled by other awesome rocky snow mountains, like a king surrounded by his queen and ministers. At the foot of this range lies a valley famous as a retreat for meditators. The air is redolent with the fragrance of herbs and mountain freshness. Workers, toiling endlessly, have dreamed of visiting this place. In this peaceful and beautiful forest grow flowering willows, blossoming rhododendrons, beech, pines, and many wild flowers. There is a waterfall, like white silk scarves hanging. The sound of falling water is inviting.

Near the waterfall stands a simple stone house, uncluttered by ostentatious ornament. It blends easily into the rocky landscape. Inside, the pillars and beams are of cedar. In the front, a large window opens on to a porch. Blue smoke once lifted gently from the chimney and disappeared into the sky. Here lived a famous scholar. His room was completely lined with books. He enjoyed the beauty of nature and was competent in the fields of philosophy, art, medicine, and poetry. He spent all his time in taking long walks and in reading and writing. Occasionally, dwelling in retreat, he suppressed memories of work and struggle in his earlier life in the cities. He treated his servant-disciple in a fatherly manner, but with a certain measure of pride and disdain, which insured his obedience and efficiency. He instructed his disciple in all matters, from how to brew tea and cook food to the fine points of philosophy. His servant never spoke to him, for his time was taken up with listening to the scholar.

Once they took a walk, and his servant warned him that the bridge they were about to cross was unsafe. But the scholar would not listen. For an answer, the teacher said, "The scope of my vision is much greater than yours." As he trod on the bridge, it collapsed and he died in the turbulent river.

In the pure land of the beautiful snow ranges
Lived a learned man, a poisonous flower with
    venom-nectar.
The disease of pride turned him deaf and dumb.
On hearing a word of advice, he committed suicide.
A man foolishly wise is like a leper;
A wisely foolish man is like a baby learning to walk.
To ride the horse of knowledge, it is necessary to
    have a saddle.

Aphorisms

You bought it from your father, you sold it to your
    mother,
You shared the profit with friends;
Thieves can't steal this wealth—
Your family heirloom is arrogance.

When the scholar's head rots
His nose becomes deaf.
It's the fault of the blind students
Who fail to see his head.

The lecture of the newly appointed teacher
Sounds like a general's orders.
It's the fault of the senior students
For asking profound questions.

Mistaking a charlatan for a savior
And offering him one's life with blind faith
Is like falling asleep on a borrowed horse:
The horse will return to its owner.

The restless poet who composes
A verse in praise of mountain solitude
Is like a criminal turned judge
Writing a textbook on law.

The insight which transcends mind
And the mind which activates awareness
Are like a healthy youth
Who has good eyes and legs.

The Nameless Child

There is a mountain of gold. When the sun's rays strike it, it is irritating to look at. It is surrounded by red, green, yellow, orange, pink and liver-colored clouds, wafted gently by the wind. Around the mountain fly thousands of copper-winged birds with silver heads and iron beaks. A ruby sun rises in the East and a crystal moon sets in the West. The whole earth is covered with pearl-dust snow. Upon it a luminous child without a name instantaneously comes into being.

The golden mountain is dignified, the sunlight is
    blazing red.
Dreamlike clouds of many colors float across the sky.
In the place where iron birds croak,
The instantaneously-born child can find no name.

Because he has no father, the child has no family line. Because he has no mother, he has never tasted milk. Because he has neither brother nor sister, he has no one to play with. Having no house to live in, he cannot find a crib. Since he has no nanny, he has never cried. There is no civilization, so he cannot find toys. Since there is no point of reference, he doesn't know a self. He has never heard spoken language, so he has never experienced fear.

The child walks in every direction, but does not come across anything. He sits down slowly on the ground. Nothing happens. The colorful world seems sometimes to exist and sometimes not. He gathers a handful of pearl dust and lets it trickle through his fingers. He gathers another handful and slowly takes it into his mouth. Hearing the pearl dust crunch between his teeth, he gazes at the ruby sun setting and the crystal moon rising. Suddenly, a whole galaxy of stars wondrously appears and he lies on his back to admire their patterns. The nameless child falls into a deep sleep, but has no dreams.

The child's world has no beginning or end.
To him, colors are neither beautiful nor ugly.
The child's nature has no preconceived notion of
    birth and death.
The golden mountain is solid and unchanging.
The ruby sun is all-pervading.
The crystal moon watches over millions of stars.
The child exists without preconceptions.

Haiku

The beginner in meditation
Resembles a hunting dog
Having a bad dream.

His parents are having tea
With his new girlfriend—
Like a general inspecting the troops.

Skiing in a red and blue outfit,
Drinking cold beer with a lovely smile—
I wonder if I'm one of them?

Coming home from work,
Still he hears the phone
Ringing in the office.

Gentle day's flower—
The hummingbird competes
With the stillness of the air.

A flower is always happy

A flower is always happy because it is beautiful.
Bees sing their song of loneliness and weep.
A waterfall is busy hurrying to the ocean.
A poet is blown by the wind.

A friend without inside or outside
And a rock that is not happy or sad
Are watching the winter crescent moon
Suffering from the bitter wind.

Glorious Bhagavad-Ghetto

Hawk is silly
Because of its hawkishness,
Good is bad
Because of its goodishness.
Bad is so good
Because of its bluntness.
Raven vulture lizard
A monk a nun
A dog a cat
Venerable mosquito
Sick frog
Healthy guinea pig
Giant grain of sand—
They all speak a mutual language:
Who we are
What we are
Maybe we are
The neighbors might know about us.
Do the neighbors know the Tantra?
What is Tantra?
Is black black?

Thanks be to the wise or the stupid,
Mrs. Jones

Mr. McLean.
Glory be to the rain
That brought down
Concentrated pollution
On the roof of my car
In the parking lot.

Literal Mathematics

Zero is nothing
One is bold
Two is loneliness
Three is the other
Four is the peacemaker
Five is a group
Six is the parliament
Seven is a happy conclusion
Eight is security
Nine is trooping
Ten is convenient
Eleven is agitation
Twelve is helpless
Thirteen is a threat
Fourteen is a land speculator
Fifteen is a market researcher
Sixteen is the desperate
Seventeen is a troubleshooter for the ecologist
Eighteen is a silk merchant
Nineteen is a junior executive
Twenty is sportsmanship
Twenty-one is a Jewish banker—
But zero is one in the realm of oneness
Oneness is one in the realm of zeroness

Two is sixteen in the realm of eighteen
Twenty-one is glorious after the teething of the three
Sixteen is five nobody knows who they are
Seven is ten in the realm of coins
Nine is nineteen because of sharp corners
Three is eight you have chosen a bad tailor
Four is fourteen the grammar school is inadequate
Twenty is eighteen need for equitation lesson
Eleven is fifteen bad Christmas gift
Twelve is seventeen a carrot is not a radish
Thirteen is thirteen odd man out
Glory be to the six, good table manners.
Jam jar
Honey pot
Lemon sherbet
Who's kidding whom?
Kids are kite
Kites fly
Kids stumble
In the glorious desert mole-hole.
Life as it was.
Could life be?
I mean that way?
Do you really?
But zero is what?
Well . . . well, zero is.

Glory be to those who have missed aeroplane
   connections—
Fly United.

Burdensome

The best minds of my generation are idiots,
They have such idiot compassion.
The world of charity is turned into chicken-foot,
The castles of diamond bought and sold for tourism—
Only, if only they . . .
Oh, forget it.
What is the use of synchronizing?
Raccoons are pure animals, they wash their food.
Beavers are clever animals, they build their dams.
Hot cross bun is for Easter.
Men who care for themselves turn into heroes
Walking on cloud—but are not dreamers—
But performing a miracle.
Distant flute makes you happy and sad—
Only for the shepherds.
Long lines of generations are hard workers.
Glory be to the blade of grass
That carries heavy frost
Turning into dew drop.

Tibetan Lyrics

Like a hunting dog, my friend,
You are always hungry, hoping for me.
The weather is good today:
Vanish to the distant jungle.

Yesterday I did not offer you tea,
Today I ask you not to be angry;
Tomorrow, if the weather is good,
Together we will go to battle.

This black stallion of mine:
If you ride it to the plain, it is like the shadow of a
    bird;
If you ride it to the mountain, it is like a flame;
If you ride it to the water, it is like a fish;
If you ride it to the sky, it is like a white cloud.
When ornamented with a saddle, it is like a king setting
    out to battle.
This is an excellent great horse—
Out of delight and respect, I offer it to you.

When I ride a horse

When I ride a horse,
I hold my seat.
When I play with snakes,
I snap them on my wrist.
When I play with dangerous maidens,
I let them talk first.

PART FOUR

In the Land of Promises

To Britain's Health

Such sharpness
Such honesty
The world is made of truth and lie
Truth of deception
Who buys that?
Jigsaw puzzle is true
Cyclops doesn't see double-vision
World's sportsman
World's prettiest girl
Demanded by mankind of the world
Proud woman
Sharpened pencil
Peacock with dots
Hallucinogenic drugs
Golden Syrup
In the name of Her Majesty the Queen
Hollow cock
Rotten wood
Cathy McCullough at the campfire
I told you
You told me
I'm sorry I forgot
I wasn't paid for this
Humorous Jack Elias

Bob Halpern as jewel merchant
Tile of Mexico
Let us have a bullfight
Sword of prajna
Impeachment of the Buddha
Holy Dalai Lama
Quarterhorse
Mustang
Stallion
Honorable discharge
English saddle
Smell of good leather
Glory be to our Queen
Long live Elizabeth the Second
My Queen
Towards whom I feel integrity
Long live the Queen
Stiff upper lips
Pleasing British leather saddle
Equitation
Diana Judith
Union Jack
Red white and blue
Glory be to Elizabeth the Second
The rushes of Scotland
Swamps of Northumberland
The dimples of the Lake District

Plains of Salisbury
White chalky shores of Dover and Devonshire
There is something nice about our Kingdom
Glory be to Diana and her English nose
Foggy London
Confident boys
Union Jack flying
In the midst of traffic in Piccadilly
Still majestically bearing the symbol of St. George
And St. Andrew
St. Patrick
My second home
Glory be to the thistles
Clover
And the royal rose
Cockney accent
The Liverpool accent
The Midlander's
The Welsh
Scottish
And the Irish
Such rich people
Enjoying the bank holiday at Blackpool
May the Kingdom last long
May the Kingdom last long free from the Tory
The Labour
The Liberal

May Her Majesty ride on a powerful white horse
With her banner fluttering in the winds of English
   country power.

Palm is

Palm is.
It may be small but includes the universe.
Fortune-tellers make a living out of it—
Flamingos sleep on it—
Mothers slap their children—
It's for begging, giving—
When thinkers don't have thoughts, they rest their
    foreheads—
Trees that have palms invite holiday-makers—
Can a jackal read a palm?
Maybe S. C. can read,
But is S. C. a jackal?
S. C. is tricky,
But jackals are perky, with long throbbing howls.
Maybe they read their palms in the cold wintry night
In the aspen grove.
The Lord of Death supposedly reads palms
To see through your life's work:
The good man
The wicked
Banker
Priest
How many infants got slapped with a palm
How much dough we molded with our palms

How many directors clapped their palms on the table
     shouting, "Let's do it!"
I wonder whether Miss Bishop has used her palms in
     her life?
The palms of the night
To write poem of palm
Flamingos
Flamingos' mothers
S. C.
Fortune-tellers.
The earth is a big palm,
So is the sky;
Jointly they make the four seasons.
By mistake, cities grow up between their palms,
A vein of highways begins to grow,
There's no room to breathe,
People call it pollution.
I wonder what it's like to be the palm of the universe?
The stars and moons,
Saturn and Jupiter,
Mars and Venus,
Twinkle between two palms.
By fault of the palms being too tight
Sometimes various comets escape
Creating cosmic fart.
The world of fart and palms!
Goodnight, jackal.

In the land of promises

In the land of promises
One flea bite occurred.
In the midst of continental hoo-ha
One bubble occurred in a tall lager-and-lime glass.
Midst a spacious sand dune
Sand swarmed.
Lover with sweat.
Primordial egg dropped from the sky
And hit Genghis Khan's head
In the middle of the Gobi Desert.
Horny camels huffed and puffed to the nearest water.
Desert seagulls pushing their trips to gain another food.
Suzanne with her jellyfish
Volleyed back and forth by badminton rackets—
Oh this desert is so dusty
One never gains an inch
Not a drip of water
So sunny
Almost thirsty
Very thirsty
Fabulously thirsty
Terribly—
Oh it's killing me
This desert this sand
Preventing me from making love

Preventing me from eating delicious supper
With all-pervasive crunch of sand.
I wish I could go to the mountains
Eat snowflakes
Feel the cool breeze—
I wouldn't mind chewing icicles,
Making the delicious cracking sound
As I step on the prematurely frozen pond,
Making the satisfying sound of deep hollowness
As I step on the well-matured frozen pond,
The undoubtedly solid and secure sound
On a fully-matured frozen pond.
Suzanne would love that,
Because she is the punisher in the desert
And she is the companion
When we skate across this large, fully-frozen pond.
Let's fly across the ice
Let's beat the drum of our hearts
Let's blow the bagpipe of our lungs
Let's jingle the bells of icicles
Let's be cool and crispy—
Suzanne, join us!
What is gained in the hot deserty wretched sweaty
    claustrophobic sandy skull-crunching dusty world of
    Gobi?
Who cares?
Come to the mountains, Suzanne!
O Suzanne!

How small can you be?

How small can you be?
So tiny that you can't even talk or think.
How big can you be?
So big that you can't think or talk.
Desert hounds are said to be tough
But, looking at their own ancestral skulls,
They could become painfully wretched.
Come, Come, said the young woman,
Come with me to the mountains
Where the heathers, rhododendrons, tamarisks and
    snowflakes grow.
Her hair fluttered by the cool mountain air
Which is so fresh,
Her lips and eyelids quivering at the freshness she
    experiences,
Sunbeam reflecting on the side of her face
Portrays a lady of life.
As she turns her head
From the little irritation of long flowing hair
She says, Mmmm.
But on the other hand she is somewhat perturbed,
Not knowing whether she is glamorous or ugly,
Begging for confirmations right and left,
Still listening to the distant flute of her past present
    future.

Is she wretched?
Is she fabulous?
Thundering heartbeat in her chest,
Riding the horse of jealousy at a million miles a
    minute—
Could someone fall in love with her?
Could she be the world's monumental femininity?
Is she the possible hag
Who eats living chrysanthemums or dead bees?
Winding highway to the Continental Divide,
Snake coiling for its own purpose,
Tortoise carrying heavy-duty shell with meaningful
    walk,
Red silk rustled,
Hearty blue-blood aristocracy
With its blue ribbon blown in the wind
From the palace window—
Is this such a woman as deserves a coronation ceremony
    attended by the galaxies, the stars and the world of
    yes and no?
Is she such a woman as is never hampered by a dirty,
    greasy, bullfighter, manslaughtering, unworthy man?
I wonder whether she has tasted her blood
Or her nectar.
Glory be to our Queen!
Lust is for everybody, by the gallons.

Envy is for one, who picks and chooses
Like a woodpecker digging after one worm.

However, everybody's a lover—
Let's celebrate in love!

Dying Laughing

It is ironic that the pigeon got run over by a car.
It is sad that the M. C. P. people got insulted.
What's wrong with you is that you talk too much—
Or, for that matter, think.
Yesterday was a glorious day,
Today is reasonable but a bit chilly.
Boomslangs never made friends with man,
But boa constrictors swallowed a church
And assumed its shape.
Joshua Zim appreciates highlights,
Or for that matter deep throat.
Flip a coin!
Take a chance!
What is the worth of all these thoughts?
A mustache is not worth it
If there is no mustacher.
On the whole, it's a gigantic black hole
Where things come and go in and out,
Sometimes cheap sometimes extravagant.
The world is a big mind
Which reacts to all conclusions.
Scattered thoughts are the best you can do.
Let the mercury jump on a drummer's drum
Breaking and gathering—

What's wrong with you is
You think too much,
Talk;
So don't talk
Or think;
Or, not talk first,
Then don't think;
Or, don't think first,
Then talk.
But finally we find non-talker, thinker;
Non-thinker, talker.
Let's forget about it all—
Om Shanti
Shhh
But don't . . .

Do it all anyway!
Let's do it completely!
That the whole universe could be exasperated
And die laughing!

Wait and Think

Wounded son—
How sad.
Never expected this.
Oily seagulls
Crippled jackal
Complaining flower—
Very sad.
Is it?
Is it?
Is it?
Maybe a couple of doughnuts might cure
Or, for that matter, wine that is turning into vinegar.
Little flowers
Snow drops
Early bird—
Hopefully gentle breeze will turn into hurricane.
That might be somebody's wild guess.
William Burroughs' rhetoric
Single-minded
Street dogs
Thieving dogs—
Oh how fantastic this world.
Julius Caesar never made it.
Suns and moons have their problems,

The galaxies of stars have their problems among them.
Mysterious world sad and happy:
The problem is that we are too serious.
Gurdjieffian literal thinking
Theosophical secrecy
Maroon car
Defective door
Glorious in the name of one-upmanship.

Does His Holiness sneeze?
Does His Holiness cough?
If he does,
Who doesn't?
If he doesn't,
Who does?
Truth of the matter is
We are a gigantic spider
Constantly weaving webs
But never giving birth.
Who is not brave enough to swallow the sun
Eat the earth
Bathe with the galaxies?
Let us join this feast
Free from orgy and ritual.
Hallelujah!

Missing the Point

Brain hemorrhage
Sick pigeon
Trust in the heart
Good soldier
Neat girl in the cosmic whorehouse—
Our minds becoming bigger and smaller
As if they were Lynn's mustache
Which gets bigger and smaller as he talks.
Stalagmite stalactite
Mutual love affair—
Today I rose relatively early.
My thoughts are constant
Like a leak in an old castle
Plop plop plop ploo plop.
Things go on—
Suddenly a nasty thought,
Deep sigh;
Pleasant thought,
Longing sigh.
The chatters of Hasprays continue like subconscious
    gossip.
Does mind speak?
Does mind walk?
Sometimes walk speak,

Speak walk.
Who is instigating all this?
Maybe the uranium that makes atom bombs
Shooting star
Allegorical presentation of the dharma
Historical confirmation of the
    antidisestablishmentarian sophistication of the
    seemingly sane society of the past.
July Fourth
Flash of fireworks—
At the same time,
Lingering thought tells me
My private secretary is really drunk.

Nitpicking
Farfetched—
This rock is problematic:
If it were arranged,
It could complain to the artist;
But since it is not,
No one to sue.
Expectation of the future is too much.
Glory be to somebody's cow dung,
It is too lucid to blame.
There goes everything
Down the drain.

1135 10th Street *(and G.M.)*

How nice it is to meet an old friend,
How refreshing to see an old friend;
Meeting an old friend is much better than discovering
    new ones—
Passing an old stone
On the winding mountain road,
Passing an old oak tree
In the English country garden,
Passing a derelict castle
On the French hillside,
Passing an old ant
On the sidewalk—
Glory be to Giovannina!
Maybe all this is a castle in the air,
Maybe this is my conceptualized preconceived
    subconscious imaginary expectation,
Maybe this is just a simple blade of grass.
It is all very touching.
Maybe it is just glue,
Glorified glue
That glues heaven and earth together,
Glue that seals great cracks in the Tower of London.
However,
There is something nice about Giovannina:

When she smiles,
She cheers up the depressed pollution;
When she talks,
She proclaims the wisdom of precision.
She is somewhat small,
But dynamite.
She seems to know who she is.
She could create thunderstorm;
She could produce gentle rain.
She could get you good property;
She brings down the castle in the air.
She is somehow in my opinion well-manufactured.
Fresh air of the Alps—
I think she is fresh air,
Which turns into a well-cared-for garden
Free from lawn mowers and insecticides.

1111 Pearl Street *(and D.S.)*

Our anxiety,
Our case history,
Our problems with the world—
We tried so hard to accomplish,
We tried very hard.
But now we are a sitting rock in the midst of rain;
We are the broom in the closet;
We are just leaves rejected by an autumn tree.
Sometimes we think highly of ourselves—
Thundering typhoons!
Glory be to Captain Haddock,
Punished for not being crazy enough,
Sent to jail for being crazy.
Does a pitchfork have a blade?
Do the handcuffs have emotions?
Persecuted by your own guilt,
Uplifted by your chauvinism—
The whole thing is a bag full of razorblades and
    pebbles.

The Alden *(and Thomas Frederick)*

I hand you my power;
If I grow you grow.
Your childishness is the ground where you can take part
    in the power.
Your inquisitiveness is magnificent.
There is need for a further growing tie with heaven and
    earth.
I have given you the space,
The very blue sky;
The clouds and the suns and the moons are yours.
But you are confused,
You like more toys:
Should they be made of gold, or plastic?
Should they come from New Jersey, or from the
    collections of the British court?
Could you use your responsibility as a golden joke, or
    a vajra scepter?
It is very heavy,
But I think you can hold it.
Canoeing is not for you,
Maybe parachuting.
Embroidering is not for you,
Maybe executing.
You, my son,

Take your Swiss Army knife—
Make a samurai sword out of it.

Aurora 7 *(#1)*

Glorious year for my work.
Glorious diamond for my business.
Glorious gurus visited me.
What could go wrong, Chögyie?
Worlds of yes and no have their place in their Christian
    original sin,
But my world is not that—
My world of nowness where tortoises can fly,
Birds can swim.

For the first time in my life, this is final:
It is the beginning.
I never began my life before.
I struggled with tutor, policeman,
Disciplinarians with long faces, deep frowns,
Accusing of being a naughty boy right and left.
Now the significant tutor-friend I have in this city of
    Boulder
Is the sheriffdom,
Who are actually very obedient.

American democracy is falling apart.
The officialdom of democracy are embarrassed.
In the realm of ceremonies and empowerments

There is victory chatter,
There is personal pride,
There is a significant proclamation:
Chögyam was born as a peasant's kid
But he is willing to die as the universal monarch.

Whycocomagh?

Sometimes there are trees.
Sometimes there are rocks.
However, occasionally there are lakes.
Always, to be sure, there are houses.
To be sure certain, there are views of a certain
    gentleman being crucified.
Nevertheless, the deep-fried food is very decent,
So good that one almost forgets bourgeois cuisine.

The coastal sky seems to frown at us
With its benevolent threat.
We receive plentiful rain.
In green valley pastures brown cows graze.
Tibetan-tea-like rough rivers carry the highland soil.
Occasional mist and fog bring wondrous possibilities.
Naive hitchhikers laugh and scrutinize our convoy.
The highlands are beautiful, free from pollution,
The lowlands regular, telling the whole truth:
There is nothing to hide.
Harmonious province hangs together,
But for occasional economic panic.
Men of Shambhala would feel comfortable and
    confident in the province of no big deal,
Flying the banner of St. Andrew adorned with the lion
    of Scotland, red and yellow.

We find it beyond conflict to fly the banner of the
Great Eastern Sun.
It is curious to see their flags strung on yellow cords,
Nice to watch the children cycling in the ditch,
Nice to discover all the waiters serving on their first
day,
Nice to see that nobody is apologetic,
Good to see alders taking root after the forest fire of
pines.

To My Son

Be fearless and consume the ocean.
Take a sword and slay neurosis.
Climb the mountains of dignity and subjugate
    arrogance.
Look up and down and be decent.
When you learn to cry and laugh at the same time, with
    a gentle heart,
All my belongings are yours,
Including your father.
Happy birthday.

Not Deceiving the Earth *(and M. S. N.)*

In protecting the earth, we found good pine needles
    and harsh dried wood, along with rocks, helpful.
When you begin to examine our earth,
You find tiny mushrooms and small grass blades,
Ornamented by the chatter of ground squirrels.
You find our soil is soft and rocky;
It does not permit artificial soil topping.
Our pine trees are diligent, dedicated and graceful;
In either life or death they will always perform their
    duty of pinetreeness,
Equipped with sap and bark.
We find our world of wilderness so refreshing.
Along with summer's drum, we produce occasional
    thundershowers, wet and dry messages:
We can't miss the point.
Since this earth is so bending and open to us, along
    with the rocks,
We are not shy,
We are so proud—
We can make a wound in a pine tree and it bleeds sap,
    and courts us, in spite of the setting-sun shadow;
They bend and serve so graciously, whether dead or
    alive.
We love our pines and rocks.

They are not covered with the superstitious setting-sun
chemical manure of this and that.
We are so proud of the sky that we produce on our
horizon.
Our stars twinkle and wink as if they know us;
We have no problem of recognition.
Our rocks and pine trees speak for us.
I love this soil—dusty, sandy, good, and free from
astroturf:
Good earth, good grass, good pine tree, good
Newton—
So good.
We love them all.
With them, we could bring about the Great Eastern
Sun vision.

International Affairs of 1979

Uneventful but Energy-Consuming

Maybe Julius Caesar was right,
Organizing straight Roman roads throughout Europe.
Had the nose of Cleopatra been a different shape,
History might have changed.

This year is quite uneventful,
Regurgitating over and over that the nations have no
    chance to chew and eat a good meal.
The success of Joe Clark is replacement,
Adopting dog instead of cat as house pet in the
    Canadian Parliament.
Farewell to Pierre Trudeau:
His invitation to visit Tibet was comparable to the
    second visit of Nixon to China.
The pontiff's messages and declarations of good will
    are like having a pancake:
We know syrup will come along.
It is time for the Christians to unite:
Maybe the clean-shaven Catholics could join with the
    bearded Eastern church.
Margaret Thatcher's prime-ministership was
    frightening,
But turns out to be not so feisty.

We are reassured that she decided to wear a skirt as
   opposed to trousers—
What a relief!
Tories always tame ladies,
And the Liberals and Labour party wish they had a she-
   leader who could wear riding breeches.
However, England will be always England:
When she is sad, she becomes tough;
When she is tough, she becomes soft.
Good old glory is fading,
And now they refer to the kingdom as ruled by
   Britannia, as opposed to Elizabeth the Second.
We are sad at the death of Uncle Dicky;
He was such a good person, but he had to pay his
   karmic debt:
Instead of being killed on board the ship *Kelly*,
He was destroyed on a fishing boat—
May he be reborn as a Shambhalian warrior.
Vietnam invasion of Cambodia,
China invasion of Vietnam:
All of those jokes are comparable to a group of lizards
   biting each others' tails.
Where is the spirit of communism?
Marx, Engels, Lenin—
If they returned and saw what a mess they made in the
   universe, they would be horrified.
We find nobody is practicing true communism.

The Chinese declaration of religious freedom in Tibet
   is humorous:
You are free not to practice religion!
And the Panchen Lama beckons the Dalai Lama.
Opening the door of Sino-Tibetan tourism fooled the
   sharpest and most professional journalists;
They lost their critical intelligence.
Islamic tradition is fantastic:
"Killing enemy, develop wealth in the name of Allah."
The grand Ayatollah declares spiritual principles in the
   name of hate,
Recapturing the example of *Jaws.*
Sino-American declaration is sweet and sour,
Missing the Hunan beef of Mao Tse Tung,
Both parties not knowing how to handle their power.
Taiwan takes secret delight that it does not have to
   maintain international law and order.
Korea lost its leader,
Park killed in a parking lot by his own security guards;
Unifying South and North Chao Xian to make Korea
   out of Korea is questionable.

In short, the nations are capitalizing on what they were.
In turn, they lose what they are.
This year is not an exciting year at all,
In spite of short dramas and quick exchanges.
There could be an exciting perspective to it:

Declaration of war between Islam and the rest of the
faiths.
The Shah as *le chat* got out of the bag,
Terrified, frustrated—we feel sorry for the Empress
Farah.
We realize that the United Nations is a rib cage
without heartbeat or lungs,
Trying to do its best.
In spite of China being chairman of the Security
Council,
Nothing gets done.
We are sad—
It is hopeless.
We are happy—
We could contribute.
The state of affairs of the world is somewhat better
than a male dog pissing on an appropriate bush.

Seasons' Greetings

Emerging to the surface,
Such virginity
Blossoming as a teenager—
Wish I was Spring's father.

As the thunder gathers rain,
Flowers drink water;
Arrogant greenery has no hesitation.
Summer provides festivity, and life is worth living.

Hot pregnant mother
Preparing the eggs and sperm for the next year,
So voluptuous and ostentatious.
O Autumn, I will never go to bed with you,
But you, come to dinner with me!

Constriction and rigidity of your martial law do not
    frighten me.
You give me chills and shivers.
But the way you decorate the mountains—
I admire your extravaganza.

PART FIVE

Love's Fool

The Perfect Love Poem

There is a beautiful snow peaked mountain
With peaceful clouds wrapped round her shoulders.
The surrounding air is filled with love and peace.
What is going to be is what is,
That is love.

There is no fear of leaping into the immeasurable space
    of love.
Fall in love?
Or, are you in love?
Such questions cannot be answered,
Because in this peace of an all-pervading presence,
No one is in and no one is falling in.
No one is possessed by another.

I see a beautiful playground
Which some may call heaven,
Others may regard it as a trap of hell.
But, I, Chögyam, don't care.
In the playground beautiful Dakinis are holding hand
    drums, flutes and bells.
Some of them, who are dancing, hold naked flames,
    water, a nightingale,
Or the whole globe of earth with the galaxies around it.

These Dakinis may perform their dance of death or
    birth or sickness,
I am still completely intoxicated, in love.
And with this love, I watch them circle.
This performance is all pervading and universal,
So the sonorous sound of mantra is heard
As a beautiful song from the Dakinis.
Among them, there is one dakini with a single eye,
And turquoise hair blown gently by the wind.
She sends a song of love and the song goes like this:
    HUM HUM HUM
    If there is no joy of Mahamudra in the form,
    If there is no joy of Mahamudra in the speech
    If there is no joy of Mahamudra in the mind,
    How would you understand
    That we Dakinis are the mother, sister, maid and
        wife.
And she shouts with such penetrating voice, saying
    Come, come, come
    HUM HUM HUM
    Join the EH and VAM circle.

Then I knew I must surrender to the dance
And join the circle of Dakinis.
Like the confluence of two rivers,
EH the feminine and VAM the male,
Meeting in the circle of the Dance.

Unexpectedly, as I opened myself to love, I was
  accepted.
So there is no questioning, no hesitation,
I am completely immersed in the all-powerful, the
  joyous Dakini mandala.
And here I found unwavering conviction that love is
  universal.
Five chakras of one's body filled with love,
Love without question, love without possessions.

This loving is the pattern of Mahamudra, universal
  love.
So I dance with the eighty Siddhas and two thousand
  aspects of Dakinis,
And I will dance bearing the burden of the cross.
No one has forsaken me.
It is such a joyous love dance, my partner and I united.

So the clear, peaceful mountain air
Gently blows the clouds,
A beautiful silk scarf wrapped round.
The Himalayas with their high snow peaks are dancing,
Joining my rhythm in the dance,
Joining with the stillness, the most dignified movement
  of them all.

Early Outward

Get up today! The sun is shining brightly.
Listen! You are the essence of my heart,
The goodness of life.
I invite you. Get up today!

Today is gone very quickly, tomorrow will come.
Please do not give up your hope
That we will have time to taste
Happiness and sorrow.

If you are the moon in heaven,
Show me your face as full moon!
If this is the season of summer,
Show me the rhododendron flowers!

On the mirror of the mind
Many reflections could have occurred.
However, the face of the beloved one
Cannot be changed.

If the heart has any pattern,
There can be no change.
Will the sun rise tomorrow?
It is useless to ask such silly questions.

Whether the sun arises or not,
I don't make any distinctions.
My care is only for you,
That in your heart the genuine sun should rise.

If she is my dearly beloved one,
She should be called "One Who Has Stolen My
  Heart."
The dance of apparent phenomena—
Mirage: is this performed by you?

When I meditate in the cave,
Rock becomes transparent.
When I met the right consort,
My thought became transparent.

Dearly beloved, to whom my karma is linked,
I could not find anyone but you.
The wind of karma is a force
Beyond my control.

This good aspiration and karma
Are impossible to change:
Turbulent waterfall of Kong Me—
No one can prevent it!

When my mind recalls the dearly beloved,
There is no shyness or fear:
Majestic dakini that you are—
This must be my good karma!

Does love kill anybody?

Does love kill anybody?
What is the sound of one hand clapping?
Love is not a burden, my dear!
Poetry is not a burden for the true poet.
The notion of "chain"—
The notion of "blade"—
Flowers
Honey
The moon
Chrysanthemums
Sweet smile
Teenager
College kids
Sharpened pencil
Incense sticks by the dozen
Red ribbons in your hair
Coca-Cola advertisements which speak of "action"
Sportsmanship
Skiing in the snow
A red pullover
Drinking cool beer—
Be a sportsman in a unisex outfit,
Sky-blue with red passion-stripes,
Go-go person with wings on your sneakers,

Intercontinental cosmopolitan sportsman getting into
    the love—
More poetry
More literature
Tokyo
Cairo
New Delhi
Taj Mahal
Paris
Blond hair of Oslo
Blond mule
Blond Pekingese—
Arabs brew good coffee
But stabbing each other with a jewel-inlaid hack knife
    is another matter.
Love by telephone.
Writing a love letter is creating a mistress.
Bachelor creates mistress by making a date.
Mind's duplicity—
Run
Kick
Philosopher
Technocrats
Autocrats—
Are bound by a unilateral declaration:
Money is no object.
What the wind sweeps—

What the fires burn—
I fall in love
Because love falls into me at home.
Rock is not loveable,
But its not-loveableness is loveable.
Take a thistle to bed
And make love to it.

Love's Fool

Love.
What is love?
What is love.
Love is a fading memory.
Love is piercingly present.
Love is full of charm.
Love is hideously in the way.
Explosion of love makes you feel ecstatic.
Explosion of love makes you feel suicidal.
Love brings goodliness and godliness.
Love brings celestial vision.
Love creates the unity of heaven and earth.
Love tears apart heaven and earth.
Is love sympathy.
Is love gentleness.
Is love possessiveness.
Is love sexuality.
Is love friendship.
Who knows?
Maybe the rock knows,
Sitting diligently on earth,
Not flinching from cold snowstorms or baking heat.
O rock,
How much I love you:

You are the only loveable one.
Would you let me grow a little flower of love on you?
If you don't mind,
Maybe I could grow a pine tree on you.
If you are so generous,
Maybe I could build a house on you.
If you are fantastically generous,
Maybe I could eat you up,
Or move you to my landscape garden.
It is nice to be friends with a rock!

Report from Loveland

First you like your neighbor,
You have a friendly chat;
Then you are inquisitive,
You begin to compare;
After that you are disturbed
By a lack of harmony;
You hate your neighbor,
Because there are too many mosquitoes in your house.
How silly it is to have a territory in love.
The trouble with you is
That you have forgotten your husband;
The trouble with you is,
You have forgotten your wife.
"Oh this love of datura
It's killing me
But I like it
I would like to keep on with it—
One late night
Drove home
Having been loved
Oh how terrible to be at home
It's chilly
Unfriendly
Feels guilty

But angry
Household articles
Begin to talk to me
My past
My home affairs
My love affair
My wife my husband
Oh shut up!
It's none of your business
You stove
Just get out of my way
You rug
Make yourself invisible
I'm not going to tidy you people up
But
But
But
It's my home
I always want to have a home to come back to
Hell on earth
Hungry ghost
Jealous gods
Human passion
Euphoria of the gods
Stupor of the animals
I thought I was having fun
I'm so innocent

If only I could be with my lover
Nothing would matter
But
The past is haunting me
If I could live in the present
Constant fountain of romance
Nothing would matter
How foolish
How stupid—
Maybe how fantastic."

It all boils down to
Rotten fish beef stew gone bad.
Before we imitate the cuckoos or the pigeons,
We had better think twice
Or thrice.

1018 Spruce Street *(and K.A.)*

So passionate
That your lips are quivering
So angry
That your blood is boiling
So stupid
That you lost track of your nose

So much so
In this world of so-so
So much
Therefore so little
So little
So great
Just so

The beauty lies in
A rose petal
Just touched by
Melting morning dew
Beauty lies in
Dragonflies
With their double wings
Buzzing neatly
As if they were stationary

Beauty lies in
Majestic shoe
That sits diligently
While the meditators
Torture themselves
In a restless shiver

So right
Norwegian girl
With her occasional professorial look
Dancing with the typewriter
Wife-ing
Just so
With her lukewarm iron
How titillating
(This ticklish world)
Just so

If you're going to tickle me
Be gentle
Be so precise
That I could be amused
But wouldn't get hurt
By your clawing
But titillating enough
To stimulate my system
With your feminine healthy shiny

Well-trimmed nail
Just so.

The trees
Grow
Just so
Baby ducks
Learn to float
Just so
Mosquitoes' beaks
Well-made
Just so

Oh you Norwegian girl
Do you know how many warts
On a toad's back?
How many wrinkles
On granddad's forehead?
How many deals
Steve Roth has made?

Nothing to worry
Everything is
Just so
Doesn't quite hurt
But sometimes
Painfully ticklish.

78 Fifth Avenue

It was a desolate space you provided today;
It was hearty, but sadly WASP.
The subtle air of power is devastating
In the midst of the Black Velvet advertisement.
It is a rewarding experience that you are not on a
    billboard,
But a breathing human being
Who produce a star on your nose as you sweat.
Our meeting was like a lady rider having a chat with a
    horse in its stall
With the atmosphere of potent dung, refreshing hay,
While the neighboring horse, clad in a tartan blanket,
    looked on.
This desolate concrete cemetery that you claim is your
    birthplace—
I feel you deserve more than this:
Rebars and concrete facades,
Eternally farting cars spreading pollution,
Yellow cabs producing their own aggression for the
    sake of money and legality—
You should be sitting on rocks
Where the heathers grow, daisies take their delight,
    clovers roam around and pine trees drop their
    needles of hints.

You deserve a better world than what you have.
I would like to take you for a ride in my world,
My heroic world:
We ride in a chariot adorned with the sun, the moon
   and the four elements;
We take a great leap as we ride;
We are not timid people;
We are not trapped in our beauty or profession.
Oh you—
Your corrupted purity is still immaculate from a
   layman's point of view.
However, I am not a layman:
I am a lover.
Let us chew together a blade of chive—
You could take me out for dinner next.
Heaven forbid!
Gosh! as they say.
Suddenly I miss you.
Do you miss me?
You miss
I miss
You miss
I miss
You miss
I miss
Should you miss me?
Should I miss you?

It's all a mutual game.

If you miss me, maintain your is-ness.

When I see you next, I want to see you exactly the same
as I saw you now.

But that is too foolish—

Let us come to an agreement:

If I miss you, you will be slightly different;

If you miss me, I will be slightly different.

Let us meet each other in our growth and aging.

In any case, let us build the Empire State Building on
top of the Continental Divide.

Off Beat

In the clear atmosphere, a dot occurred.
Passion tinged that dot vermilion red,
Shaded with depression pink.
How beautiful to be in the realm of nonexistence!
When you dissolve, the dot dissolves.
When you open up, clear space opens.
Let us dissolve in the realm of passion,
Which is feared by the theologians and lawmakers.
Pluck, pluck, pluck, pluck the wild flower.
It is not so much of orgasm,
But it is a simple gesture,
To realize fresh mountain air that includes the
    innocence of a wild flower.
Come, come, D.I.R., you could join us.
The freshness is not a threat, not a burden.
It is a most affectionate gesture—
That a city could dissolve in love of the wildness of
    country flowers.
No duty, no sacrifice, no trap.
The world is full of trustworthy openness.
Let us celebrate in the cool joy,
The turquoise blue,

Morning dew,
Sunny laughter,
Humid home.
Images of love are so good and brilliant!

When a cold knife is planted
in your heart

When a cold knife is planted in your heart,
What do you say to it?
When you have swallowed a cold stone,
What do you say to it?
When you have swallowed a cold icicle,
When you feel love hurts,
What do you say to it?
This kind of hurt, is it pleasurable?
Pain pleasure
Pleasure pain
Cold hurt
Hurt cold
Hurt hot
Hot hurt—
Wish I had never experienced blue sky or green grass,
Beautiful lover (would-be).
Would such hurt, gut hurt, throat hurt, brain hurt, lung
    hurt, such hurt hurt,
Bring about cosmic love affair one of these days?
Maybe the bleeding part should be served as dessert,
With occasional bubble, occasional odor
And occasional music played with it.
Such hurt love is so love love hurt.

Maybe frogs have never experienced this;
The Pekingese, the poodles are lucky
That nobody killed themselves being lovesick.

You hurt
You tingle me
You tingle hurt
Hurt tingle
Tingle hurty
Hurt tingly
Pain
Lust
Love
Passion
Red
Ruby
Blood
Ruby lust
Lust cold
Cold ruby
Frozen rose
Rose frozen
Lust passion
Cold hate
Hate ruby
Passion lust cold hate ruby
Hot ruby lust

Flute hot
Lust flute
Cold icicle
Hot ruby lust passion cold flute
Pure
Pure ruby
Pure hot cold ruby
Lust passion pure cold ruby
Cheat
Hot cheat
Cheat convert
Hot passion cheat
Cheat blood
Cheating blood
Passion ruby flute
Cold hot flute
Play
Hot play
Cheat play
Cheat play hot passion ruby
Drum
Thunder
Thunder drum
Drum thunder
Hot drum hot cheat
Hot cheat ruby drum
Drum drum drum

Cheat drum ruby
Cheat hot passion
Ruby hot piss
Flute
The flute
Throbbing flute
Throbbing heart
Cheat throbbing heart
Hot cheat throbbing passion flute
Throbbing sex
Passion ruby
Deaf
Mute
Mute passion
Deaf passion
Throbbing deaf mute passion in cold ruby liquid.

Dixville Notch

A glowing worm is said to be brilliant,
But the brilliant sun is more convincing.
Sweet smile seems to be the best,
But genuine affection is more convincing.

When I was riding with you
On that winding road of our mutual snow mountain,
You said, "Oops!"
I said, "What?"
Nonetheless we are both fascinated and intrigued by
    our mutual trip,
Fueled by immense passion and a glowing sense of
    humor.

We might find snowdrops somewhere.
You said you didn't like the melting snow,
You said you liked the fresh snow.
I was intrigued by the way your constructive mind
    worked.
While gazing at an icicle,
At first a little one on its way, melting,
You then discovered that little one becoming bigger.
Such rediscovery of the phenomenal world and
    appreciation of detail—

Indra and Brahma and Avalokiteshvara
Would have found this appreciation so sweet and
    glowing.

When we met,
You were merely there;
When we talked,
You were tongue-tied.
And again when we met,
You were more than there;
When we talked,
You were very articulate.

Our mutual guess became like the dance of the
    dragonfly:
You guessed,
I guessed;
Did anybody guess?
Did anyone guess?
Sometimes one wonders whether we should give away
    this mutual secret to anybody.

Spring gives way to summer
And summer gives way to autumn.
Autumn gives way to winter.
Then we are back to square one,
Watching icicles again.

When you are attacked by this and that,
You should hold the needle of nowness
Threaded with our mutual passion.
When you are hungry and fearful of the small big
    world,
You should look at the Great Eastern Sun
With the eye of our mutual passion.
When you are lonely,
You should beat the drum of sanity
With the stick of our mutual passion.
When you feel awkward,
You should drink the sake of confidence
With the lips of our mutual passion.
When you feel you are nobody,
You should hold the falcon of great humor
With the hand of our mutual passion.
When you feel spoiled,
You should fly the banner of genuineness
With the wind of our mutual passion.

You should have no problem in propagating our mutual
    passion
As long as
Or as short as,
A journey's been made
In the name of the biggest,
Or the smallest,

Which transcends eruption of stomach.
Peacock
Magpie
Wolf
Rattlesnakes equipped with antennae
Jackal
Polar bear
Shaggy dog
Taj Mahal
Good wasabi
Chicken feet
Rothman's Special—
All of these, wicked and workable, are our world.
Including all those there is no problem,
Whether the so-called phenomenal world is sweet or
    sour, painful or pleasurable.
We should make sure that we do not put them in the
    oven
And make a convenient loaf of bread of them.
Let us not regard the world as one,
Or, for that matter, let us not regard the world as
    multiple.
As long as we dance and sing, sweep the floor, wash the
    dirty dishes
And celebrate in the name of satin silk diamond ruby
    emerald and pearls,
Fresh water clinking with ice,

We are producing rich cold powerful ideal world,
With a touch of warmness:
Let us project to this universe our mutual passion!

If I may go further:
We are not deaf, not dumb,
We are not mute.
We are the world's best possible goodness,
Outspoken, exaggerated, understated fanfare,
With the goodness of goodness.
The wicked will tremble and the good will celebrate.
Impossibility is accomplished in the realm of
    possibility—
Fathomless space being measured.
Depth of passion being explored.
Let us eat snail adorned with fortune cookies.
Let us drink amrita fizzed with our mutual humor.
Let us ride the horse of delightful disestablished world,
Saddled with our mutual passion.

Did you know the sun rises in the east?
Don't believe those who tell you that the sun rises in
    the west.
Shall we have our mutual celebration?
One who fights is eternally poor.
One who shares is victorious.
Let us celebrate in our mutual passion!

I Miss You So Much

I miss the Regent
And that transforms into clarity,
The luminosity which perpetually lights itself:
No need for switch or kindling wood.
I miss my son
And that transforms into energy,
Unyielding energy and play
Which can perform the cosmic dance.
I miss my queen
And that transforms into the power of speech,
Utterance of genuineness and nowness
Which cuts thoughts and proclaims the vision of
    indestructibility.
I miss the princess consort
And that transforms into passion;
Every moment becomes coemergent twist—
It is beyond coming or going.
The pain of the delight
Lights up the universe.
Choicelessly I remain as flaming vajra.

Bon Voyage

Bon Voyage.
You go away.
You go away with doves and rhododendrons.
You fade away in the memory that is part of the blue
    sky.
You will be forgotten with ashes of burning cigarettes,
As if fossils never formed in the prehistoric age.
Happy birthday to you.
You fade away in my life.

PART SIX

Victory Chatter

Garuda Is the Mighty Force

Garuda is the mighty force of creation and destruction.
He acts unerringly and will not hesitate.
The children of Shambhala will follow the pattern of
    his swooping and wheeling
And the two opposing forces will come to balance one
    another in perfect harmony.
This is the future of mankind.

The Wind of Karma

Who killed my only father?
Who killed my only mother?
Who caused the rain of blood?
Who gathered the black clouds of the thunderbolts?
Who caused the earthquake that shook the whole
     world?
I asked these questions in the middle of a crowd
But no one was able to answer.
So I asked a second time and a third,
Shouting at the top of my voice.
My mind was blank and I didn't know what to think.

Suddenly the great red wind of karma arose.
The king of death appeared on the face of the earth
And raised a fearful hailstorm.
The flag of no-retreat, emblazoned with the knot of
     eternity,
Unfurls before the storm.
Even the wind of karma takes delight in blowing it.
The truth of the pattern emerges
And unshakable confidence is aroused.
Now I am certain,
I am fearless,
There is no retreat:
The voice of truth is heard throughout the world.

Victory Chatter

As an old soldier
Watching the territory:
Flags go up and down
Where the soldiers gather;
Hearing distant archery contests;
Horses are unsaddled in the meadow;
Flute of a soldier who is in love;
Listening to the creaking of the cannon swayed in the
    wind.
The sound of the flute fades away;
The banner of victory is fluttered by the breeze;
Rustling of armor takes place constantly.
Occasional smell of horse dung,
Occasional cheerful chatter of the armed force—
I bide in the tent, the general,
Listening to the occasional grasshopper's leap:
How grateful to be a soldier!
Ah! storm rises,
Gold-black cloud in the southern quarter—
I can hear the flag fluttered violently by the wind.
A thought occurs to me:
"Somebody's getting out of the administration."
And another:
The memory of a whistling arrow on the battlefield

And the high-pitched echo of swift swordsmanship.
A thought occurs to me:
"Somebody's getting into business,"
As the horses begin to neigh—
They are ready for tomorrow's battle:
"Somebody's going to teach philosophy tomorrow
And get out of the administration at the end of the
    week."
The cloud from the south moves close to the center of
    the sky,
Dark with wrath.
We hear resounding deep thunder.
The warriors' fight must go on—
Vigor and bravery
Sharp sword
Well-cared-for bows and rustling armor
Are our only resources.
Frontier warfare is sad and happy,
It is romantic and treacherous.
Oh! How I feel that I am a good soldier,
A good general,
Listening to the rustling of armor
Where the white tents are blown by the wind.
We are sharpening our swords and our arrowheads.
How romantic to be fighters
Conquering the American plains!
Good luck to Boulder

Rock
The Rocky Mountains
The pine trees—
Full of fantastic battlegrounds.
The kingdom rests at eleven and eleven.
It is good to fight,
It is good to know that victory is,
It is good that I alone can wage this particular warfare.
Sharpened sword
Arrowheads
I fight in the old fashion.

Aurora 7 (#2)

Sun is dead,
Moon is born;
Moon is dead,
Sun is born.
Who said that?
Which is true.
Sun-moon are alive,
Sun-moon are dead;
They both shine on their own schedules.
Chögyam is alive;
No hope for the death of Chögyam—
Taking care of Chögyie
With hot warm towels
Breakfast in bed
Chamber pots in their proper places,
Serving Chögyie as the precious jewel who may not stay
    with us—
All take part in the platitude of serving Chögyie as a
    dying person!
Oh! What's become of Chögyie?
He drinks too much,
He's bound to die soon—
Taking care of Chögyie is no longer would-be mother's
    pleasure?

Thriving strongly,
Existing powerfully,
Eternally growing,
Stainless steel veins:
Chögyie is a crystal ball with stainless steel veins,
With diamond heart.
Even the most accomplished samurais' swords can't cut
    Chögyie's veins,
Because his veins are vajra metal,
The blood is liquid ruby.
The indestructibility of Chögyie is settled—
For foes very frightening:
Downfall of him never occurs;
For friends rejoicing:
Chögyie is made out of vajra nature.
Such good Chögyie makes people shed their tears;
Such good Chögyie makes people tremble before his
    vajra dignity.
Chögyie is going to be pain and pleasure for all of you,
Whether you hate or love him.
Chögyie's indestructibility could be venom as well as
    longevity-nectar.
Here comes Chögyie,
Chögyie's for all,
Take Chögyie as yours—
Chögyam says: Lots of love!
I'm yours!

Memorial in Verse

This year of building the kingdom:
Dealing with the four seasons,
Studying how millet grows,
And how the birds form their eggs;
Interested in how Tampax are made,
And how furniture can be gold-leafed;
Studying the construction of my palace—
How the whitewash of the plain wood can be dignified,
How we could develop terry cloth on our floor,
How my dapöns can shoot accurately,
How my financiers can rush themselves into neurosis,
How the cabinet session can arrive at pragmatic
    decisions.
Oh, I have watched the sky grow old
And the trees become younger as the seasons changed.
I have experienced the crisp air of December and
    January becoming a landmark of my life
As twenty grey hairs grow on my head.
I have witnessed that I have grown older and old,
As I grasp the scepters and handle the rice heaps,
Performing ceremonies.
I have thought I have also grown younger every day,
Taking showers, looking at myself in the mirror—
Perky and willing, I see myself:

That my lips don't quiver, my jaws are strong,
My gaze is accurate.
When I think of this year,
The most memorable occasion was the explosion of
    love affair,
Which was no joke.
It is true, I think of that every day
When I take my Aldactone and my Reserpine for my
    good health,
As prescribed by the physicians.
I think of my love affair as I wipe my bottom
Sitting on the toilet—
One appreciates that yellow dye sitting on white paper
As it flushes down the efficient American plumbing
    system.
One of this year's highlights is also that I failed and
    accomplished a lot:
The failure is mine, the accomplishment is to my
    Regent.
Sometimes I think of the Ganges and Brahmaputra, or
    the Yellow River;
I could have shed many tears.
And I think of the glaciers of Mt. Everest;
I could become solid, steady and stern.
I have developed the face of a frozen glacier.
So my life comes and goes,

The same way the swallows sway back and forth in the
air.
They may catch flies or they may not.
I have developed the jurisdiction and fair constitution
of the Kingdom of Shambhala.
I have told the truth of the Great Eastern Sun vision
from my moldy lips.
I have experienced certainty within uncertainty,
Because one realizes the traffic of ants does not have
traffic lights
And it is hard to give them speeding tickets.
My journey grows and shrinks as the Vajracarya and
the Sakyong,
The first of the Kingdom of Shambhala's history.
However, the wicked will tremble and the awakened
will rejoice.
I have fought, ambushed, raped, attacked, nursed,
abused, cultivated, fed, nourished, hospitalized my
world
With its world-ees.
Now I have grown very young and very old.
I appreciate the sun and moon, snow and rain, clouds
and deep blue sky;
I appreciate the ruggedness and the beauty of the
universe,
Which is sometimes cruel, developing sharp thorns of
cactus,

And sometimes produces chrysanthemums of fantastic
 scent.
Blood or ink: both I take as yellow and purple color.

Maestoso Drala

When we met, I felt that you were the essence of lha.
You frighten me.
If you are the agent of the lha,
Have I been corrupted too much to ride on you?
Am I worthy?
Have I been spoiled and corrupted by drinking Coca-
    Cola?

You accepted me so kindly,
Therefore I named you Drala.
You have the muscles of Vajrapani,
You have the neck of a true Mukpo,
You don't walk, but you dance.
You are not my dream, you are reality—which frightens
    me.
You are capable of projecting the true windhorse—
Maybe I have forgotten how to ride windhorse truly.
You are kind and gentle, with extraordinary gait.
Your steps can't be measured by the horses of Magyel
    Pomra.

When we held the big race in order to gain the throne
    of Gesar of Ling—
Do you remember?—you were there as the steed of
    Gyatsa.

When we swam across the river of Ma in a suit of
armor,
Many comrades were killed but you were fearless.
As we forded the river—do you remember?—you came
out pink
Because of your whiteness and the enemy's blood in the
water,
And you proclaimed yourself with three neighs of Ki
Ki So So as a warrior horse.
When we defeated the hordes of Hor—do you
remember?—you were there.
As we marched into the city of the anti-dharmic world,
Your gait was magnificent,
But you were so energized by the clinking of our suit
of armor to kill the basic rudra,
We had to slow you down,
So that we could enter into the city in a threatening
and dignified way.
When we teamed together in the cavalry,
You were there as Yuja, destroying the swiftness of the
barbarians.
I remember very clearly how your white coat was
stained by the blood of the enemy
As we slashed their bodies, separating the limbs from
the torso.
We rode together and looted the enemy's camp
And you were heightened with the smell of the blood
that stained the sword of your rider.

You went after the enemy and we had to restrain you,
Because killing too many enemy is bad taste:
We have to conquer rather than kill them.
But your gait was wonderful, maintaining your
    terrifying *passage*,
White as you are.
We fought many times,
With your help overcoming the barbarian insurgents.

I welcome you back to my world,
European as you are, known as Maestoso bloodline:
I never betrayed you as the strength of Mukpo.
I have no doubt that you will not have any difficulty in
    relating
With the fluttering of our victory banner and listening
    to our anthem.
And I am sure you will remember the trooping of the
    colors of our Kasung.
As you are known as Drala, maintain your arrogance.
I love you.
Be my companion, at war or in peace.

Trooping the Color

Hold the rein of meagerness.
Ride on the saddle of forward vision.
Control the horse of uncertainty.
Make your decision with a good seat.
Our government will proceed like good cavalry.
As you ride watch out for the mole holes,
So that none of the riders fall off this victorious horse.
In short, ride the horse with profound frown and smile.
Do not forget that you have a bow on your right and a
    quiver on your left.
Fight this world of setting sun with a joyous war cry.

Good Morning within the Good Morning

Because of my forefathers,
Because of my discipline,
Because my court, the tutors and the disciplinarians,
    have been so tough with me,
I feel enormous gratitude to them:
They taught me the Shambhala vision.
Instead of sucking one's thumb,
You taught us to raise head and shoulders.
With sudden unexpected eruption,
I have been blown into the cold land of a foreign
    country.
With your vision, I still perpetuate the discipline you
    taught to me.
With second occasion of the Shambhala Training of
    Five,
I would like to raise a further banner for the students
    and their practice:
May we not suck our habitual thumbs,
May we raise the greatest banner of the Great Eastern
    Sun.
Whether tradition or tales of the tiger,
We never give up our basic genuine concern for the
    world.
Let there be light of the Great Eastern Sun

To wake up the setting sun indulgence.
Let there be Great Eastern Sun in order to realize
Eternally there is always good morning.

Haiku

Claws of the lovely child,
Beauteous smile of the magnificent woman—
Both are eating raven's shit,
Experiencing the taste of the one flavor.
Walking with deer foot,
Trotting like a horse,
Biting like a butterfly—
Aren't we all fooled by the universe?
Catching the rain of blood,
Appreciating the dew drops of winter and spring—
Aren't we all appreciative, enjoying the great bliss?
The mirage of antelopes caught in the trap of religion,
The fish of discursive thoughts caught by the net
    without hooks and worms—
Aren't we joyful that we catch samsara without
    aggression or militaryhood?
Our generals are very kind,
Our military strategy is very kind,
We never shoot anybody but we capture them—
Our only concern is, can we feed them all?

In this glorious catch and kill,
Cure or kill,
I would like to dedicate my experience of being in
    Chateau Lake Louise to Lady Jane,

Who is the best of the pigeons of the peacocks,
The best of the jackals of the snow lions,
The best of the lizards of the turquoise dragons,
The best of the ducklings of garudas.

All goes well.
Ki Ki—all goes worthywhile—so so!
I take pride in our expedition.
Since my mother left me without her fur chuba
I decided always to be chubaless,
A warrior without wearing clothes, walking in the cold.
My mother and my guru have agreed on this principle,
So now I am furless, clotheless.
On the other hand I remained king,
Sitting on a throne with a self-snug smile.
If I never had heritage,
This never would have happened:
Thanks to Gesar
And anybody related to the Mukpo family
Who has had the delicious meal of the Mongolian
    meat-eaters.
Good dish,
Solid gold brocade,
Genuine suit of armor,
Riding on a white horse into battle—
We take pride in all of those.
Ki Ki So So!

Ki Ki So So to Lady Jane!
Ki Ki So So to my white horse!
Ki Ki So So that we are the warriors without ego!
Om svabhava-shuddhah sarva-dharmah svabhava-
    shuddho ham.
Ki Ki So So!

Turning Point

Learning is difficult.
Growing up is painful.
Conquering is arduous.
Discipline is endless.

With your exertion and dedication, sooner or later
You will learn how to swallow the sun and moon
Together with a galaxy of stars.
You will learn to ride the tiger.
You will fly with the banner of the Great Eastern Sun.
Come along and join us!

Cheerful birthday, my son.
You should supersede your father.
May the wisdom of the Rigdens be with you on this
    occasion.
May the blessings of the Kagyü and the Nyingma
    lineages guide you forevermore.

Command

Nuclear catastrophe is imminent.
Man's aggression to kill himself or others is imminent.
Tiger hates his or her stripes and is going to untiger.
Yet Karmapa never left a declaration of independence.
The Kagyü kingdom is intact,
If not totally packaged by Vajradhatu of North
    America.
I am so sad, so devastated,
I feel I have lost my head.
But I have gained a new head, a Karmapa head.
For better or worse I will rule according to Karmapa's
    imperial command:
I will remain as the Emperor of Kalapa.
We still allow people to smile and grin:
Human beings' habitual patterns are obviously the best
    of their ability to create a society of their own,
Whether they are tiger, lion, yak or buffalo.
We like America in its buffaloness.
Let America be buffalo kingdom, in spite of the
    unicorns!
Cheerio! as we say in Britain.
You deserve your cheerfulness, nonetheless.

Golden Sun

For Shibata Kanjuro XX, Archery Master

In this land of *kami-no-yama*, I still miss you.
We are all longing for your wisdom.
As you know, we have lost our leader the Karmapa,
But it is comforting to have you as good friend and
    teacher.
The mirror has never stopped reflecting,
The *kiku* has never stopped blossoming.
Yumi still twangs,
Ya still fly.
Our students constantly practice and look forward to
    your further teaching.
I, your friend, am getting old and sick,
But still my heart's blood turns into liquid iron.
The strength of appreciation for the warrior heritage
Is part of my metallic blood,
And my bones are made out of meteoric iron.

Profound respect to you, Sensei, on your birthday.
May the Great Eastern Sun continuously arise in your
    life, with happiness and prosperity.

How to be Old Shambhalians
and Youthful Propagators of Shambhala

Burning trees produce smoke.
Kings who will become kings produce burning trees.
Queens who will become would-be queens produce
    small brooks.
Wood chips hit the rocks.
Nonetheless, ministers would sweep gently in the air
As they choose what kind of trees they should blow:
Aspen, tamarisk, rhododendrons, pine, birch.

The kingdom settles as peasants delight in their
    lambing season,
Foals bounce around,
Warriors sharpen their swords in the mountain brook,
Bowmakers look for yak horn and willow bark,
Highlanders with their greasy, weathered smile discuss
    the season
But produce an abundance of butter and cheese,
Lowlanders darkened by the sun's stroke work with the
    ripening grain.

The people of Shambhala rejoice,
Learning that their children will pick up greater wisdom

In the midst of short pine trees and rocks
    weatherbeaten from the ocean.
Constant rain and mist are no disturbance in the life of
    Shambhalians.

We occasionally welcome foreign visitors.
Economically we are self-centered:
Shambhalians are the great merchants who travel across
    the rest of the world.
Fearing no one, we exchange oil for water, diamond for
    agate, wool with silk.
Because we self-exist, Shambhalians have no fear or
    hope.

I am so happy and proud to be the first subject of
    Shambhala.
May the Great Eastern Sun pervade our nation.
May we have no fear of who we are.
May we know who we are, and accept our intelligence.
Victory to Shambhala!
May the Great Eastern Sun arise.

Child's Concept of Death

Warriors die and are born.
So do swallows die and are born.
In this blue sky—
Sun shines,
Moon sets,
Anything could happen.

May the rhododendrons never die.
Juniper should not die.
I will die one day,
Maybe without knowing.

The Meek

Powerfully Nonchalant
and Dangerously Self-Satisfying

In the midst of thick jungle
Monkeys swing,
Snakes coil,
Days and nights go by.
Suddenly I witness you,
Striped like sun and shade put together.
You slowly scan and sniff, perking your ears,
Listening to the creeping and rustling sounds:
You have supersensitive antennae.
Walking gently, roaming thoroughly,
Pressing paws with claws,
Moving with the sun's camouflage,
Your well-groomed exquisite coat has never been
    touched or hampered by others.
Each hair bristles with a life of its own.
In spite of your feline bounciness and creeping slippery
    accomplishment,
Pretending to be meek,
You drool as you lick your mouth.
You are hungry for prey.
You pounce like a young couple having orgasm.
You teach zebras why they are black and white.

You surprise haughty deer, instructing them to have a
    sense of humor along with their fear.
When you are satisfied roaming in the jungle,
You pounce as the agent of the sun.
Catching pouncing clawing biting sniffing—
Such meek tiger achieves his purpose.
Glory be to the meek tiger
Roaming, roaming endlessly.
Pounce, pounce in the artful meek way,
Licking whiskers with satisfying burp.
Oh, how good to be tiger!

PART SEVEN

Sacred Songs

Supplication

O Karmapa, lord and knower of the three times,
O Padmakara, father and protector of all beings,
You transcend all coming and going.

Understanding this, I call upon you—
Give thought to your only son.
I am a credulous and helpless animal
Who has been fooled by the mirage of duality.
I have been fool enough to think that I possess my own
    projections,
So now you, my father, are my only refuge,
You alone can grasp the buddha state.
The glorious copper-colored mountain is within my
    heart.
Is not this pure and all-pervading naked mind your
    dwelling place?
Although I live in the slime and muck of the dark age,
I still aspire to see it.
Although I stumble in the thick, black fog of
    materialism,
I still aspire to see it.

The joy of spontaneous awareness, which is with me all
    the time,

Is not this your smiling face, O Karma Padmakara?
Although I live in the slime and muck of the dark age,
I still aspire to see it.
Although I stumble in the thick, black fog of
    materialism,
I still aspire to see it.

At glorious Taktsang, in the cave
Which can accommodate everything,
Samsara and nirvana both,
The heretics and bandits of hope and fear
Are subdued and all experiences
Are transformed into crazy wisdom.
Is not this your doing, O Dorje Trolö?
Although I live in the slime and muck of the dark age,
I still aspire to see your face.
Although I stumble in the thick, black fog of
    materialism,
I still aspire to see your face.

The corpse, bloated with the eight worldly concerns,
Is cut into pieces by the knife of detachment
And served up as the feast of the great bliss.
Is not this your doing, O Karma Pakshi?
Although I live in the slime and muck of the dark age,
I still aspire to see your face.

Although I stumble in the thick, black fog of
    materialism,
I still aspire to see your face.

In the boundless space of nonmeditation
He who performs the great dance of mahamudra
Puts a stop to thoughts
So that all acts become the acts of the guru.
Is not this your doing, O Tusum Khyenpa?
Although I live in the slime and muck of the dark age,
I still aspire to see your face.
Although I stumble in the thick, black fog of
    materialism,
I still aspire to see your face.

When the current of thoughts is self-liberated
And the essence of dharma is known,
Everything is understood
And apparent phenomena
Are all the books one needs.
Is not this your doing, omniscient Mikyö Dorje?
Although I live in the slime and muck of the dark age,
I still aspire to see your face.
Although I stumble in the thick, black fog of
    materialism,
I still aspire to see your face.

The kingdom of no-dharma, free from concepts,
Is discovered within the heart.
Here there is no hierarchy of different stages
And the mind returns to its naked state.
Is not this your doing, O Rangjung Dorje?
Although I live in the slime and muck of the dark age,
I still aspire to see your face.
Although I stumble in the thick, black fog of
    materialism,
I still aspire to see your face.

The father guru, the embodiment of all the siddhas,
Is all-seeing and all-pervading.
Wherever you look, his transparent body is there,
And the power of his blessing can never be diminished.
Although I live in the slime and muck of the dark age,
I still aspire to see his face.
Although I stumble in the thick, black fog of
    materialism,
I still aspire to see his face.

Living, as I do, in the dark age,
I am calling upon you, because I am trapped
In this prison, without refuge or protector.
The age of the three poisons has dawned
And the three lords of materialism have seized power.
This is the time of hell on earth;

Sadness is always with us
And unceasing depression fills our minds.

The search for an external protector
Has met with no success.
The idea of a deity as an external being
Has deceived us, led us astray.
Counting on friends has brought nothing
But sorrow and insecurity.
So now I have no other refuge
But you, Karma Pakshi, the lotus-born.

Think of us poor, miserable wretches.
With deep devotion and intense longing
I supplicate you.
The time has come for you to arouse yourself and do
      something.
The tradition of meditation is waning
And intellectual arguments predominate.
We are drunk with spiritual pride
And seduced by passion.

The dharma is used for personal gain
And the river of materialism has burst its banks.
The materialistic outlook dominates everywhere
And the mind is intoxicated with worldly concerns.
Under such circumstances, how can you abandon us?

The time has come when your son needs you.
No material offering will please you
So the only offering I can make
Is to follow your example.

Four-armed Mahakala

HUM!
From glorious Mount Malaya,
From the red field in the blood lake Koka,
From the charnel ground of Matram Rudra,
I invite the great protector.
Like a rain cloud adorned with lightning,
Please enter this place of practice.
SAMAYA JAH!
The vajra mahakala
Is savage and terrifying.
Holding a hooked knife with your first right hand,
Holding a skull cup of blood with your first left hand,
Brandishing a sword with your second right hand,
Thrusting a khatvanga with your second left hand,
You, the warrior with a tiger skin round your waist,
Are surrounded by your retinue, with the Raven-
    Headed One among them.

In accordance with your vajra oath
Proclaimed before the great Trungpa, Künga Namgyal,
At the hermitage of Dorje Khyung Dzong,
Protect the heart teachings of the Kagyü.
The evil beings with two tongues who pervert the
    dharma

And delight in disrupting the teachings—
Eat them as your food, O black protector.
By the fierceness of your compassionate wrath,
Instantly accomplish the karmas
Of pacifying, enriching, magnetizing, and destroying.
Lead the faithful holders of the Practice Lineage
To the state of Vajradhara.

OH MAHAKALAYA DEVA-RAKSA SAMAYA HO BALIM TE
    KHAHI!

Purifying and Invoking the
Four Directions

This pure water I pour in order to purify this ground:
With the blessings of the Rigden Father may it be
    cleansed of the pollution of the barbarian world.
Let this water be genuine nectar of the Sakyong
Who delights in the four seasons and in prosperity:
May the four quarters be cleansed.

Arise! Arise! Tiger of the East.
With six smiles on your body, you are so meek.
Please protect us and inspire us,
So that your fire can consume the coward.

Arise! Arise! Dragon of the South.
Inscrutably you play with the turbulent river;
You become the cloud of perpetual thunder.
With your wrath let us subjugate the enemy.

Arise! Arise! Garuda of the West.
Your outrageous cry wakes up the poisonous snake, to
    become your meal.
Let us conquer the setting sun world
With your wings of celestial metal.

Arise! Arise! perky Lion of the North.
You walk on cloud,
You claw the sun and moon.
With your regal turquoise mane, spread gallantry to us.
With your dignity, let us leap from mountain to
    mountain.

Invoking the Rigden Father

O Rigden Father,
Your grace and gentleness have saved us from the
    depressions of the barbarians
And your sweet smile has produced chrysanthemums.
As we watch each petal grow we rejoice and cry,
And the tears of our crying produce future warriors.
When we finger the sword blade we become
    heartbroken—
Why, with such sharpness, Rigden Father, are you not
    presently with us?
From the pain of our heartbreak we cry, Ki Ki So So!
Remembering your brush stroke, we swoon
And collapse into your overwhelming genuineness.
Watching occasional rain drops spotting your robe as
    it ripples in the wind makes us thirsty,
But you turn our thirst into elegance.
Watching your windhorse galloping in the fields about
    your palace, we feel so jealous—
Why could not we be one of your horses?—
But that jealousy turns into confidence.
Watching you do archery, we feel intimidated—
The whistling arrow hitting the target, you have such
    accuracy—
But intimidation becomes fearlessness:

We are your arrows adorned with Garuda's feathers.
O we long for you, Rigden Father!
Please bless us on this auspicious occasion!
Let our wedding be as yours;
Let us bathe in milk and honey:
Let us eat your spicy food:
We vow to perpetuate your world.
Thank you!

Invoking the Mother Lineage

We pay homage to the Mother Lineage.
Your robe is soaked in water,
Your hair is elegant and airy,
Your perfume is exquisite.
From a grain of barley dropped on the ground by
    seeming accident,
Great prosperity has sprung.
Your milk feeds the nation.
We like the crescent moon on your hair.
We emulate your openness and bounty.
You speak softly but your command carries weight.
Please do not stop loving us!
We bathe within a grove of bamboo.
Please help us to become gentle and tough!

The Education of the Warrior

That mind of fearfulness
Should be put in the cradle of loving-kindness
And suckled with the profound and brilliant milk
Of eternal doubtlessness.
In the cool shade of fearlessness,
Fan it with the fan of joy and happiness.
When it grows older,
With various displays of phenomena,
Lead it to the self-existing playground.
When it grows older still,
In order to promote the primordial confidence,
Lead it to the archery range of the warriors.
When it grows older still,
To awaken primordial self-nature,
Let it see the society of men
Which possesses beauty and dignity.
Then the fearful mind
Can change into the warrior's mind,
And that eternally youthful confidence
Can expand into space without beginning or end.
At that point it sees the Great Eastern Sun.

Meek

The warrior who is meek
Is friendly to himself and merciful to others.
Ordinary preoccupations and activities
Have never stolen his mind away.
Since he is always modest,
He is never bloated with the poison of arrogance.
Just like a tiger in its prime,
He walks slowly with mindfulness.
Since the warrior's mind is great and vast,
He sees even farther than the sky.
Since he possesses tremendous exertion,
He accomplishes his purposes easily.
Gain, victory and good fame
That warrior leaves far behind.
Because he trusts himself,
He has no need to convince others by deception.
Since his confidence has never deteriorated,
He need not be fearful of others.

Inscrutable

The warrior who is inscrutable
Is like space which cannot be punctured by an arrow.
Since he has obtained mind which is beyond mind,
He is like a turquoise dragon playing in space:
He can never be fathomed by anyone at all.
He is the water of all waters;
He is the fire of all fires;
He is the wind of all winds;
Therefore he is the warrior of all warriors.
Beyond external manifestations,
In the inner space of vastness,
The warrior enjoys the dance.
That inscrutable warrior
Gains both temporal and spiritual victory.

Enriching Presence

Rouse yourself in wearing good clothes:
This brings elegance and confidence.
Rouse yourself in eating good food:
This frees from timidity and brings fitness of body.
Rouse yourself in drinking deathless amrita:
This intoxicates you with fearlessness.
When you give rise to conviction in enriching-presence,
Your appearance is beautiful and your muscles full,
Your gait is good and your gestures graceful;
You delight in wholesome deeds,
Wise in discarding unwholesome ways.
When enriching-presence comes to the body,
You have health and increase of richness.
When enriching-presence comes to the speech,
Your tongue is eloquent and your words have power.
When enriching-presence comes to the mind,
You have humor and fearlessness.
In this ocean of butter and gold of great enriching-
    presence
The warriors of Shambhala enjoy themselves.

Song of the Self-existing Four Elements

So ya so ya!
O Tise Gangkar, in the upper province,
Welcome, great lha of the snow mountain!

The great lha is surrounded by his retinue
Like light dawning from the sun,
Praising to the heights the white glory.
The great lha is master of the sky.

You do not approach—you dawn
Like a rainbow appearing in the sky.
You do not approach—you manifest
Like a turquoise mist appearing
From the neck of a white glacier.
You do not approach—you blossom
Like flowers blossoming in a meadow.

Great lha, Peaceful White Light,
On the fifteenth day your smiling face
Is like a full conch moon in the sky
Surrounded by a host of stars.

The self-luminosity of auspicious coincidence
Arises on the earth.

The ground is filled with white light.
Auspicious coincidence is not arranged—it coincides.
In the emptiness of the formless sky,
This song of the welcoming of auspicious coincidence
Is not sung by anyone—it resounds in the heavens.

In the heavens white clouds billow.
No one creates them—they are self-arising.
They arise by auspicious coincidence.
The earth overflows with treasures of six grains.
No one creates them—they arise spontaneously.
They too arise by auspicious coincidence.

This is the good time of all auspicious coincidence.
This is the time when the gate to the arising of
    happiness opens.
Welcome Peaceful White Light!
Good! Good!
LHA GYAL LO!

Afterword

Looking into the world
I see alone a chrysanthemum,
Lonely loneliness,
And death approaches.
Abandoned by guru and friend,
I stand like the lonely juniper
Which grows among rocks,
Hardened and tough.
Loneliness is my habit—
I grew up in loneliness.
Like a rhinoceros
Loneliness is my companion—
I converse with myself.

[*Looking into the world*]

Chögyam Trungpa Rinpoche wrote these lines in Scotland in November of 1969. He was thirty years old and
at the nadir of his career. It had been ten years since he
fled his homeland in the face of materialist, totalitarian
armies bent on destroying the age-old culture that had

189

blessed him with its profoundest wisdom and highest privilege, training him to serve as a spiritual prince. A few months earlier he had "blacked out" at the wheel of his car (drunk, we may guess) and suffered a near-fatal crash that left him permanently paralyzed on his left side. He took this as a message. His response: to abandon his Buddhist monk's robes and his monastic persona and to elope with a beautiful English teenager. Such behavior outraged and alienated Western patrons as well as friends and colleagues in the Tibetan community. It was a bleak time. And, as he had done several times already in his young life, Trungpa was preparing to leave behind everything familiar, except for his sixteen-year-old bride, and cross the great water to an unknown continent.

It was a nadir from which he would rise during the next ten years to become one of the most original and influential figures in the transfusion of Eastern influences into Western life that made the 1970s a defining cultural moment. By 1976, from his headquarters in Colorado, Trungpa was writing:

> Glorious year for my work.
> Glorious diamond for my business.
> Glorious gurus visited me.
> What could go wrong, Chögyie?

> [*Aurora 7 (#1)*]

Yet despite the triumphs and the recognition and the very real accomplishments, the rhinoceros of loneliness was never far from Trungpa's door. It was the existential ground to which he returned again and again. Nowhere is this more clear than in his poetry. Loneliness is the touchstone at the back of all the masks or personae that Trungpa puts on over the years as he continually reinvents himself, from "stray dog" to "wild duck" to "hailstorm," "sharp bamboo dagger," "general," "king," "ship sailing through icebergs," "tiger," "flaming vajra," to the poignant image of an aging king taking his medications "as prescribed by the physicians," and reviewing past successes and failures from his porcelain throne as he observes "that yellow dye sitting on white paper / As it flushes down the efficient American plumbing system."

Trungpa Rinpoche was remarkable in his total lack of need for solitude; indeed there was virtually not a moment, asleep or awake, when there were not others in his immediate presence—students, attendants, lovers, administrators. His tolerance for the constant proximity of others with their hungers and "colorful trips" was perhaps a product of his training in the close quarters of the monastery, as well as of his vocation as a bodhisattva. Behind it, though, one sensed that he had early on learned how to be "alone with others," that indeed he never departed from his own essential aloneness.

This was why he could do the most private of things in the presence of others, such as composing out loud the intimate utterances of his poems, with no sense of inhibition or interruption.

From a Western point of view, we may suppose that Trungpa's loneliness began at birth when his father abandoned the family, though Trungpa himself regarded this as a normal feature of the nomadic peasant culture into which he was born (and another father soon appeared). A more drastic severing of natural human bonds (again, from a modern perspective) was his removal from his native place and his mother's daily care at the age of two to be raised in the male cloister of the monastery. In any case, at age nineteen he was violently ejected from the matrix of a basically medieval society and began a journey into adulthood, not without friends and supporters along the way, but fundamentally alone in the challenges he faced and embraced to alchemize a coherent world view from the elements of radically divergent cultures.

In one of his most triumphant poems Trungpa asserts:

> There is a significant proclamation:
> Chögyam was born as peasant's kid
> But he is willing to die as the universal monarch.
>
> [*Aurora* 7 (#1)]

This is perhaps the ultimate expression of loneliness, transformed from total deprivation to total self-possession. The transformation is akin to Yeats':

> When such as I cast out remorse
> So great a sweetness flows into the breast . . .
> We are blest by everything
> Everything we look upon is blest.

Trungpa elsewhere describes what he calls the "king's view," the sense of elevation that permits one to survey all of space and time and feel sovereign of one's own life and its possibilities. In much of Trungpa's poetry we feel him being the artist-king, vividly imagining, "finger-painting" as he liked to say, an ideal world and his own ideal presence in it. A supreme if rather shocking example of such imagining, mixing myth, memory, and desire, is the poem addressed to his horse, "Maestoso Drala."

Yet poetry is also a refuge for Trungpa, perhaps the only place where he is able to step out of all the roles and self-inventions and speak truthfully from—and to—his own heart:

> Wounded son—
> How sad.
> Never expected this.

[*Wait and Think*]

Through his poems he gives voice to vulnerabilities, pain, disappointment, and anger. This emotional honesty is the "open secret" of Trungpa's poetry that will especially reward his many devotees, I think, if they will grant Rinpoche his loneliness and his personal struggles and listen to the poems with an ear free from preconceived idealizations. By way of example, look at a snippet from the intensely devotional poem called (revealingly) "Exposé," in which—in the same breath—Trungpa both doubts himself and one-ups the normally sacrosanct forefathers of his teaching lineage:

> At least look at us the way we are,
> Which may not be the most you expect of us,
> But we have the greatest devotion,
> Beyond your preconceptions.

These are sentiments one would have looked long and hard to find expressed elsewhere, not only in Trungpa's formal teachings but even in his intimate conversation. That they can be found in his poetry constitutes a revelation, and a gift of his essential humanity from a leader who over the years progressively diminished his availability for simple human exchange and elevated his persona into the realm of the superhuman.

If loneliness is one touchstone of Rinpoche's poetry and nature, passion is the other:

Let us dissolve in the realm of passion,
Which is feared by the theologians and
   lawmakers.
Pluck, pluck, pluck, pluck the wild flower.

[*Off Beat*]

Authentic presence in the space of our lives, Rin-poche instructs, is only achievable through a passionate contact, and a dissolving, with the raw energies of life—the brilliant, the irritating, the stuff that doesn't conform to hope or expectation. Seamus Heaney speaks of "Big soft buffetings that come at the car sideways / And catch the heart off guard and blow it open." In Rinpoche's car, the buffetings are as likely to be acid as soft:

Glory be to the rain
That brought down
Concentrated pollution
On the roof of my car
In the parking lot.

[*Glorious Bhagavad-Ghetto*]

Pleasurable or painful, the point is to touch and be touched by what Trungpa sometimes called "the real reality"—

I appreciate the ruggedness and the beauty of
    the universe,
Which is sometimes cruel, developing sharp
    thorns of cactus,
And sometimes beautiful chrysanthemums of
    fantastic scent.

[*Memorial in Verse*]

In Trungpa's world, loneliness and passion are inti-
mately connected. There is a principle of transformation or transmutation by which the feeling of lack is
alchemized into positive energy. This principle is em-
bodied in the beautiful "Invoking the Rigden Father,"
in which tears, heartbreak, thirst, jealousy, and intimidation are successively transformed into creativity, ten-
derness, courage, genuineness, and confidence. It is also
especially vivid in the poem "I Miss You So Much," in
which Trungpa names his closest human connections—
his favorite disciple, his son, his wife, his mistress—all
of whom are absent as he composes the poem, and
transforms the felt texture of his missing of each into a
strength: clarity, energy, the power of speech, passion.
He concludes:

The pain of the delight
Lights up the universe.
Choicelessly I remain as flaming vajra.

[*I Miss You So Much*]

This "flaming vajra" is the essential, transmutable and transmuting fire that animates the different guises by which Trungpa lived and manifested, infusing his passion into archetypal patterns as Teacher, Lover, Leader, Devotee, and all-purpose Sage and Cynic. All of these archetypes are summoned in his poetry. The organization of this book seeks to reflect or evoke these different energies. It is my hope that this quasi-thematic plan will assist readers, especially those with little previous acquaintance with Trungpa Rinpoche, in finding their way into the poems. Having said that, I must emphasize that the themes and the selections are entirely my own and are to a degree arbitrary, as the actual poems are living organisms that escape such editorial pigeonholing.

With minor exceptions—the initial three poems and in the final section, "Sacred Songs"—the poems in each section are arranged chronologically so the reader can gain insight into how Trungpa's style and ways of seeing and responding evolved over time. All of the poems in the first six sections were composed in English, except for "The red flag flies above the Potala," "Silk Road," "Tibetan Pilgrim," "Tibetan Lyrics" and "RMDC, Route 1, Livermore," which were first written in Tibetan. Most of the "Sacred Songs" were composed in Tibetan and translated by Trungpa Rinpoche with the assistance of the Nalanda Translation Committee (which he founded for the primary purpose of translating Buddhist texts and liturgy). The exceptions, composed directly in English, are "Purifying and Invoking the Four Directions," "Invoking the Rigden Father," and "Invoking the Mother Lineage."

Trungpa was not a technician and his poems are roughed out, not highly polished. They offer little in the way of meter or rhyme. But they build on a sure sense of rhythm, a keen ear for sounds, and an inborn delight in words and the uses and misuses to which they can be put. Trained in the *mantra-yana*, which employs pure sound as well as words as sacred instruments to evoke divine energies, Trungpa carried this method over into the secular realm. "Each word that we speak should be regarded as a gem. When we speak or talk, we should regard words as tangible rather than purely as sounds." He spoke often of the need to appreciate "the vowels and the consonants." He composed his "Sound Cycles," which modulate from pure sounds to words and from Sanskrit to English, as training exercises for the theater group he directed in the early 1970s. Much later, toward the end of his life, with a mix of schoolmasterly discipline and impish humor, he drilled students on "proper pronounciation," by which he meant the upper-class British accent (or his version of it) that he had acquired during his years studying at Oxford. He wrote a series of "Elocution Exercises" in the form of short verses emphasizing difficult (for

Americans) sounds like the slighted British *r* in the phrase "the summer odour of raw earth." Examples of both Sound Cycles and Elocution Exercises have been included here as an appendix. A more potent example of the use of sounds and words in mantra-like fashion toward secular (and sexual) ends is the long, flute-like coda of the poem "When a cold knife is planted in your heart."

Some will find Chögyam Trungpa's verse too unpolished to qualify as great poetry. Be that as it may, I believe that attentive readers will discover that it is *real* poetry. By turns thorny and tender-hearted—like Trungpa Rinpoche himself—these poems are passionate transmutations of loneliness that invite us to taste the raw and real stuff of life:

> Chögyie is going to be pain and pleasure for all
>   of you, . . .
> Here comes Chögyie,
> Chögyie's for all,
> Take Chögyie as yours—
> Chögyam says: Lots of love!
> I'm yours!

[*Aurora 7 (#2)*]

Appendix

Sound Cycles

Trishula

Trident Trishula Trident Trishula Trident Trishula
Ta Ta Tri Tri Tri
Tish Tish Tishshsh Tshshool
Tshshool Tshshool Tshshool-<u>LA</u>
Trishula Trishula shshoola shshoola
Trishula Th Th Th Th
Teeth Teeth Bite Biting-teeth Bit<u>er</u>
Bluh Bleh Blade
Blade Blade Blade Blade Blade Blade
Needle
Needle-ette
Small Needle
Point
Trident Trident Trident

NOTE: Except in English words, pronounce *T* soft, half way
between *d* and *t*. In the sixth line, pronounce *Th* as in *thumb*.
Roll the *r*'s, except in English words.

Sutra

Sssoo Sssoo Soot Soot Sootr
Sootr Sutra Soootra Sutroom
Sootroom Sootree Sootro-EE
Oo Ay Oh Oh Ay Oh Ee
Soooodj Soooodj
Junction
Sutra Junction Junction Junction
Junction Junction
Confluence Union United
Unified
United Unified Junction of Confluence
United Unified Junction of Sutra

NOTE: Roll the *r* in *sootr* and throughout this cycle.

Aham

Mmuh Mmuh-uh Uh-muh
Ha Ha Aha Aha Aham
Aham Ahammmm Mama
Ahammm Me Mmuh-ee
Ee Mmuh-ee Ee-muh Mmuh-ee
My My-yin My-yin Me My
Mine Me Me My My My Mama Mama-yin

Mama-yin Mommy My-teeth
Teeth Muh-teeth Muthuh Muth
Muth Mother Mow-ther
Owther Other Oh-mother Oh-me
Mother Mother Oh-mother
Mothers Anonymous . . .
Ah-mother Ah̲am-mother Ah̲ummuh

NOTE: The *h* is definitely an aspirated *h*. The *th* in *Muthuh* and *Muth* is the hard *th* as in *thumb*. *U* and *uh* throughout also as in *thumb*.

Elocution Exercises

Instead of Americanism
Speak the English Language Properly!

The English Monarch has a white bow,
Thoroughly splendid and monumental.
Because it serves England,
It is more than daring.

The fabulous mountain deer roams.
The hair of the black tiger is tantalizing.
The world of the blue spider is tattered.
Whether we make war or not—
Roaming in the orchard is dangerous; autumn trees are
    armed.

The vicissitudes of one's life are like drowning in a glass
    pond.
The Liberty Bell cannot be sold as a gorgeous antique.
I'm sorry to say your mother might think otherwise.

Humour and Delight with the English Language

Darling, your moustache is merely a tired signature.
A celebratory metal transplant has been cordially
    ordered from Persia.
The preparatory record was hurried.
Detail from the discourse was like gaudy city clothing.
Asian hooves crushed the tiara in the palace quadrangle.
Brocade colours of military and monastery fluttered.

Playing with the English Language

From mirror arose proclamation of dancing
    nonthought. Got it?
The summer odour of raw earth turned the falcon
    fanciful.
The role of the durable donkey slowed my motor car.
I dare say there is sword advertisement.
I adore a bird and butterscotch.

Index of First Lines

Shambhala Centaur Editions